CW00373543

Published in 2006 by
Ray Archer Photography
24 Park Drive, Forest Hall,
Newcastle Upon Tyne.
England
NE12 9JP

Tel: +44 (0)191 270 1393
Mobile: 07768 402222
e-mail ray@rayarcher.com
www.rayarcher.com

ISBN 0-9554338-0-0
ISBN 978-0-9554338-0-1

Photography: Ray Archer

All images © Ray Archer

Project Manager
Mick Tonks

Picture Editors
Ray Archer
Mick Tonks

Editorial
Adam Wheeler

Design & Layout
Ray Archer & The Ark Design

Origination & Printing
The Ark Design & Print
Tel 0113 256 8712

Special thanks and acknowledgements to:
My family, Marie, Lauren and Jack for their support, understanding and
for being able to cope well as a family when I am working away or stuck
in an airport somewhere in the world. Thanks go to Adam Wheeler for his
hard work and efforts as we work together each week. To Steven
Schreurs, Pascal Haudiquert, Daniele Rizzi, Richard Fabian and the
many other who's help on the Grand Prix trail making life that little bit
easier each and every week. The organisers of the FIM World Motocross
Championship, Youthstream and their hard working crew, plus fellow
photographers, journalists, TV crews, team managers, riders, mechanics,
truck drivers, marshals and medics. Last but not least, for keeping my
cameras and photographic equipment in the best possible shape, Brian
and Stephen at Media Service Solutions, Kish Dhayatker at Canon UK
CPS with Hans Martin Fetzer's enthusiasm and IT expertise in holding
the computers together. Thank you all.

A catalogue record for this book is available from the British Library.

Contents

Foreword by Stefan Everts   5

Mx1 & MX2 Top Five Riders   6

The Teams
Yamaha intursports Motocross Team   12
Kawasaki Racing Team   18
Martin Honda   24
Team KTM / Champ KTM   30
Team Suzuki   36
Bike it Dixon Yamaha   42
CAS Honda   44
Molson Kawasak   46
De Carli Yamaha   48
GPKR Kawasaki   50

The Bikes
Everts   Yamaha YZ450F-M   52
Strijbos   Suzuki RM-Z450   56
Leok   Kawasaki KX450F-SR   60
Barragan   KTM 450SX-F   64
Coppins   Honda CRF450R   66
Cairoli   Yamaha YZ250F   68
Rattray   KTM 250SX-F   70

MX1 & MX2 Motocross World Championship
Round 1 Zolder   74
Round 2 Bellpuig   82
Round 3 Agueda   90
Round 4 Teutschenthal   100
Round 5 Sugo   108
Round 6 Sevlievo   118
Round 7 Montevarchi   128
Round 8 Matterley Basin   136
Round 9 Uddevalla   144
Round 10 Sun City   152
Round 11 Loket   160
Round 12 Namur   168
Round 13 Desertmartin   176
Round 14 Lierop   184
Round 15 Ernee   192

MX of Nations   200
Stefan Everts the legend   208
Behind The Scenes   216
Youth Stream   230

Results   234

Foreword
MX-GP 2006

Hello everyone and welcome to this special book.

It is another small honour to be asked to write the foreword for this publication and I'm sure it will be very valuable to me in later years when I can look back in fondness at what was an incredible way to say goodbye to my career as a racer.

2006 was full of great memories. The new Yamaha allowed me to take my riding to another level and from those 15 Grand Prix there were many cherished moments. I managed to hold my emotions inside until the final stages but taking the tenth title at Namur and winning my 100th GP at Lierop were amazing days that will stand out in my mind forever.

It was my final season and I could see that my son Liam really likes motocross and enjoys coming to the races. I took him on the podium when I won my eighth and ninth titles but this year I said that I wanted him up there with me as much as possible so that we could have those last moments of my career together. He won't remember much of it when he grows up but will then be able to see the pictures and the videos and it will be a nice memento for both of us.

The photo book is a great way for people to recall places, races and faces. Ray is a great photographer and has been around for a long time in Motocross, I have worked with him before and he is well respected so I know the contents of this book will be some of the best pictures you can see from the track.

I want to give thanks to all my fans and supporters, the team and Yamaha for six fantastic years, the media for their important role, my family and especially Kelly and Liam who are so special to me.

Enjoy the book and the racing for years to come

Best wishes

Stefan Everts

MX1 Top 5
Stefan Everts

Kevin Strijbos

Steve Ramon

Ken De Dycker

Tanel Leok

MX2 Top 5
Christophe Pourcel

Antonio Cairoli

David Philippaerts

Tyla Rattray

Marc DeReuver

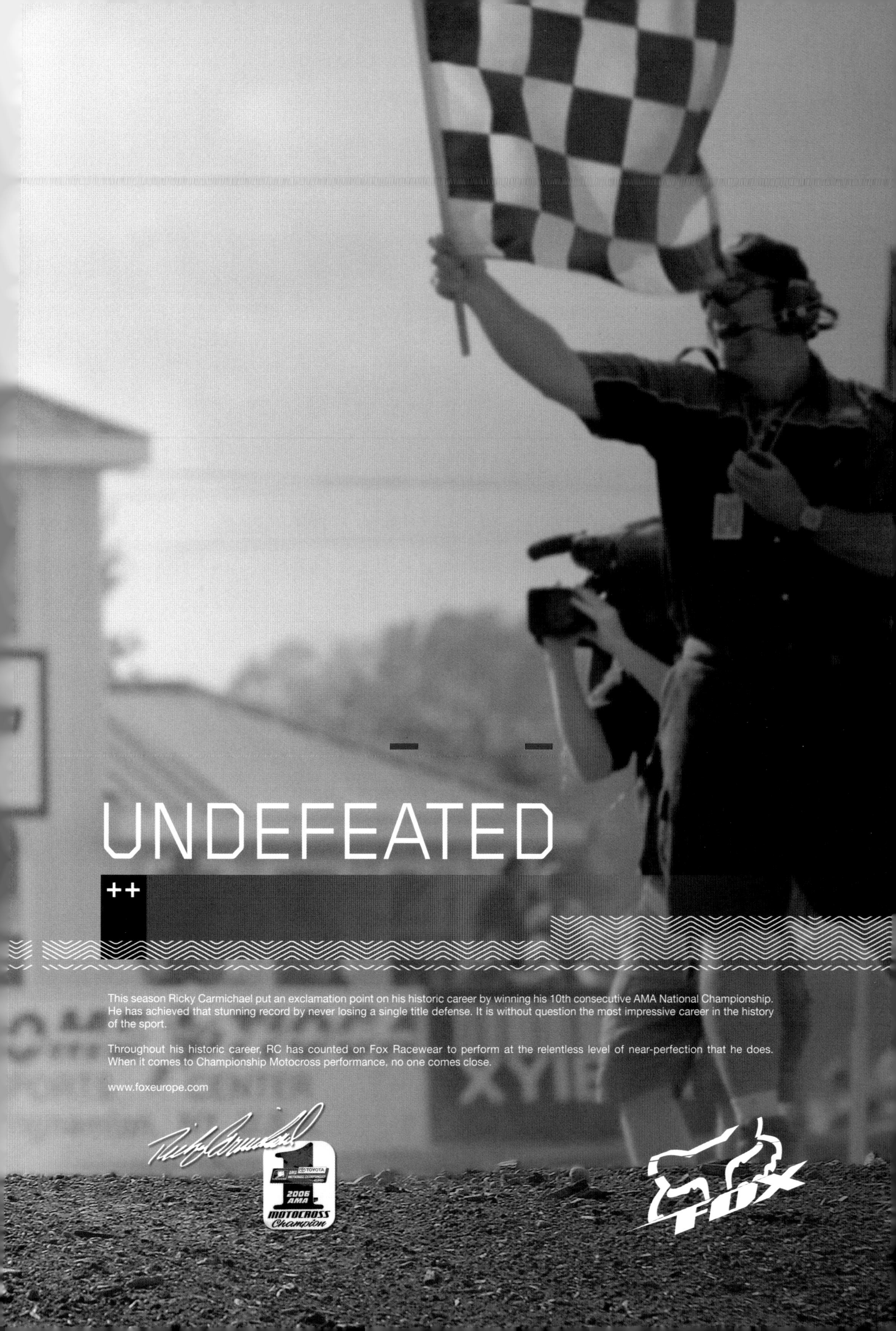

UNDEFEATED
++
This season Ricky Carmichael put an exclamation point on his historic career by winning his 10th consecutive AMA National Championship. He has achieved that stunning record by never losing a single title defense. It is without question the most impressive career in the history of the sport.
Throughout his historic career, RC has counted on Fox Racewear to perform at the relentless level of near-perfection that he does. When it comes to Championship Motocross performance, no one comes close.
www.foxeurope.com
TOYOTA
2006 AMA MOTOCROSS Champion
FOX

Yamaha intursports Motocross Team

Kawasaki
Racing Team

Martin Honda

SATURDAY MX1
FREE PRACTICE   11:00 - 11:40
FREE PRACTICE   14:00 - 14:40
TIME PRACTICE   16:30 - 17:00

SUNDAY MX1
WARM-UP   9:30 - 9:50
G.P. RACE 1   12:55 - 13:05
G.P. RACE 2   15:55 - 16:05

SATURDAY MX2
FREE PRACTICE   10:00 - 10:40
PRE-QUAL. PRACT.   12:00 - 12:40
QUAL. RACE 1   15:00
QUAL. RACE 2   15:45
LAST CHANCE   17:15 - 17:45

SUNDAY MX2
WARM-UP   9:00 - 9:20
G.P. RACE 1   11:55 - 12:05
G.P. RACE 2   14:55 - 15:05

Team KTM /
Champ KTM

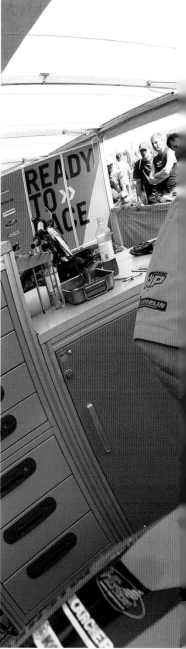

Team Suzuki

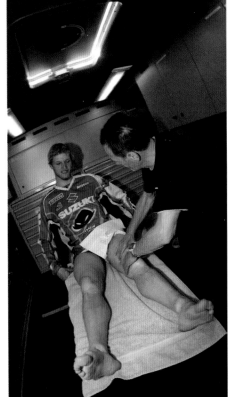

Bike it Dixon Yamaha

CAS Honda

Molson Kawasaki

De Carli Yamaha

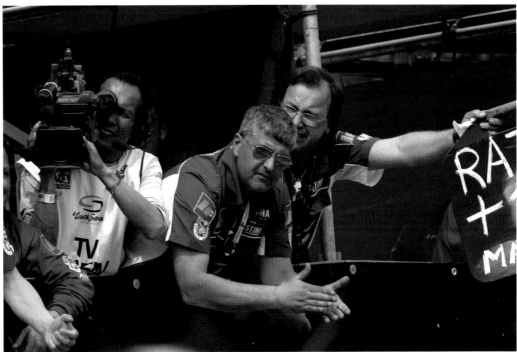

GPKR
Kawasaki

Stefan Everts
Yamaha YZ450F-M

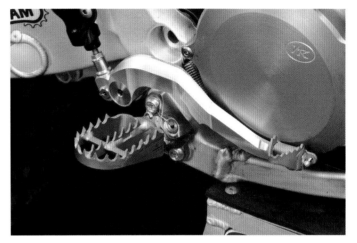

Kevin Strijbos
Suzuki RM-Z450

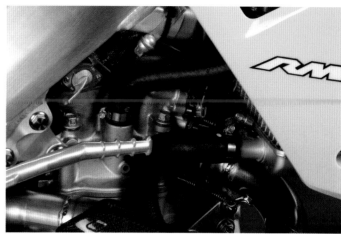

Tanel Leok
Kawasaki KX450F-SR

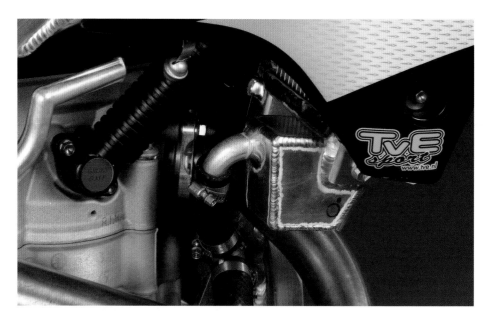

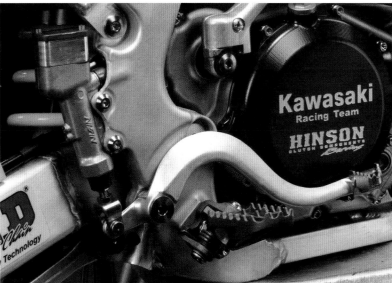

Jonathan Barragan
KTM 450SX-F

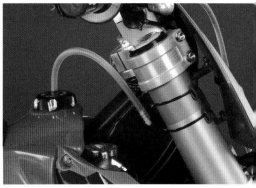

Joshua Coppins
Honda CRF450R

Antonio Cairoli
Yamaha YZ250F

Tyla Rattray
KTM 250SX-F

FIRE AND ICE

Broc "Iceman" Hepler scorched the infamous Millville whoops en route
to victory at Round 9 of the AMA Motocross Lites Championship Series.

April 1/2

R01 Zolder

R01 Zolder

Karcher Grand Prix of Flanders

The premier class of the Motocross World Championship boasted a glittering array of talent and the strongest line-up in well over a decade. The third year of MX1 (formerly the 250cc and MXGP category) opened again at the impressive Zolder circuit but by the end of a tense and muddy weekend the high-profile cast of four riders ear-marked for 2006 title success had been sliced by half.

CAS Honda's Josh Coppins had finished runner-up in 2005 and was many people's tip for a renewed challenge. The New Zealander was sadly ruled out for more than two months after hitting his right shoulder on a fence post while practicing several days before Zolder. He manfully tried to complete Saturday's schedule with heavy strapping holding the dislocation but eventually called an emotional halt to proceedings and trudged away for an operation.

Mickael Pichon was second in the 2004 series and despite a knee injury and rumours of retirement towards the end of '05 he was signed to help KTM realise their MX1 ambition. A mysterious condition that affected his heart-rate and therefore his fitness emerged over the weekend and a handful of laps in either race preceded two retirements and speculation as to whether the most successful French rider in World Championship history was also throwing in the towel for good.

Pichon was joined 'in orange' by countryman Sebastien Tortelli who was taking a one year sabbatical from an injury-ravaged seven year stint in the United States.

For months reigning Champion and Grand Prix Icon Stefan Everts had been fending off questions and debate about the 1998 250cc contest when Tortelli

and the Belgian last crossed swords, Tortelli flew over the Atlantic victorious after ending Everts' three season winning streak in the quarter-litre category. With Coppins lame and Pichon out of sorts, the spotlight became fiercer on the two protagonists and the two 35 minute and 2 lap motos at Zolder helped to re-affirm that another tight scrap was in the making. Everts had earned

a title every season since 2001 and entered the Grand Prix hot on the back of pre-season International triumphs in France, Belgium, Italy and Great Britain and raving about the new aluminium framed (with carbon sub-frame and new engine configuration) YZ 450 Yamaha. Tortelli was at last fit and by hoisting the might of KTM onto his back had the largest team and set of resources in the paddock.

The Zolder terrain was a composite of sand and earth that provided a formidable physical test. Coupled with first race nerves it was not strange to see riders picking up their machines from the damp surface. 16,000 spectators watched proceedings under a bright but changeable sky and the wins taken by Tortelli and then Everts as the duo broke away both times from the pack did little to indicate who was the livelier out of the blocks. A first moto crash by Everts gave the advantage to the KTM but the Yamaha was steadfast against Tortelli's speed later in the afternoon.

The results only offered part of the story though. The simple truth was that Everts – despite his slip – was the more comfortable of the riders. Tortelli spearheaded a new-look KTM set-up with teething problems both inside and outside of the workshop. The bike had proved delicate in winter events and the former double World Champion was riding it for all he was worth in Belgium. Other signs that Tortelli did not have the necessary package to equal Everts's speed would be swift in coming to light.

Zolder provided a career landmark for both Tanel Leok and Kawasaki. Their third position delivered maiden silverware for both the Estonian and the KX 450-F.

MX2 World Championship favourite Tyla Rattray maintained his run of Grand Prix victories after owning the last three events of 2005 after coming back from injury. The South African on his works KTM had aced every session, heat and moto in 2005 for a perfect weekend. He was not as dominant this time as team-mate David Philippaerts took advantage of mistakes by Marc de Reuver and Sebastien Pourcel for first moto glory. With two KTMs on the podium the MX2 affair was also noticeable for new Yamaha Ricci Racing rider Kenneth Gundersen notching his first top three appearance in the class since 2001 and completing his first Grand Prix for almost two years after cartilage problems.

April 15/16

R02 Bellpuig

R02 **Bellpuig**

Grand Prix of Spain

For the first time, and not the last in the remaining 13 Grand Prix, the spotlight in the MX1 class fell firmly onto the next generation as Stefan Everts played his role of the 'Piped Piper'. The Belgian would earn his second win in succession and continue his special affinity with the Bellpuig circuit.

The 33 year old won his first Grand Prix at a hot Spanish round in 2001 after two years out through injury and since then he has not looked back and not missed a title-winning party at the end of each subsequent season. This time he not only mastered the fast and dusty Catalan slopes in an authoritative second moto display but beat it's current favourite son as Jonathan Barragan gave the best ever performance by a Spanish rider at his home Grand Prix.

Barragan withheld the advances of the Yamaha pilot for a vast majority of the second half of moto1 in his defence of third position and stirred the perma-enthusiastic partisan crowd. The 20 year old was steering the '07 development version of the KTM 450 SX-F and premiered a flash of speed and maturity that would see his career hit new heights within the space of a week. Everts pipped him to the last spot inside the top three with a lap to go and set-up his score-card for the 'overall'. That the World Champion was even in such a predicament was caused by a crash coming out of the old whoops section (now two widely separated speed bumps after the FIM abolished the man-made humps from the rule book during the winter) and the exact same spot where he had launched over the bars in 2005. The incident led the occasionally superstitious reigning number one to save his white Acerbis kit for practice as the bad karma had now afforded two spills in two motos.

Kevin Strijbos claimed the race and would be the second of only two different heat winners apart from Everts for the rest of the first half of the season. He was chased again by the impressive Tanel Leok on the improving Kawasaki. Everts was truly the Grandfather of the top group with three riders in the top four all under 21 years of age. The difference in class and experience would be evident in the second foray as Everts streaked away after yet another bright start but it was encouraging to see signs of the future, post-number '72'. Everts' force after lunch would be the first moto victory in an incredible run.

Much to the KTM's dismay their once bold and mighty (not to mention costly) investment in capturing the MX1 World Championship – the only crown to elude them across the wide spectrum of off-road motorcycle racing – crumbled at only the second round. Tortelli hit the deck several times over the weekend and was struggling with an ankle he had tweaked at Zolder. The Frenchman was off the pace and wrestling the 450 manfully but was eventually outshone by his young team-mate in a surprise and unexpected addition to the script. The Pichon situation was baffling. The team announced the Frenchman's need to spend some time away from the sport before he then changed his mind and travelled to Barcelona airport. Allegedly he underwent another moment of indecision before setting foot on Spanish soil. The team had his bike prepared and ready to go but finally there was a no-show from the 2004 runner-up amid confusion. A week later and Pichon made his own statement confirming that he would indeed be stepping away from the World Championships for '06 but would continue to represent KTM in national competition within France and Germany.

Yamaha owned the MX2 class in what was a hot day of action on Easter weekend. Kenneth Gundersen won his first moto since Germany 2002 but a prang in race two allowed Antonio Cairoli to seize his first 25 points of the year. The defending Champion had fallen and hurt his already injured wrist earlier on. Despite some claims that the '06 Yamahas were not as potent as the conquering 2005 models (Cairoli, Gundersen and Billy Mackenzie, who grabbed his first podium one year after achieving his maiden moto success at Bellpuig, would all experience suspension problems in the formative stages of the season) they certainly seemed up to the task. Rattray, KTM team-mate Marc de Reuver and Kawasaki-mounted Christophe Pourcel were kept waiting in the wings as far as attention from the chequered flag was concerned. Rattray's consistency at least provided him with another overall success and consolidated his status as pre-season title favourite even though he did taste Spanish dirt briefly during the course of the opening sprint.

R03 Agueda

Grand Prix of Portugal

It was quite simply the best moto of the millennium; a clash between two riders and two styles that enthralled the public with its dynamism, tension and ultimately a dramatic finale. The first MX1 race passed by in an instant as Everts and a reenergised Tortelli somehow managed to make the other 28 riders in the class disappear. Tortelli was on a mission. A disappointing Spanish Grand Prix meant that he had five days of reflection and brief time to muse with the KTM engineers before re-launching his opposition to Everts' autonomy at Agueda.

Mercifully the rain that had plagued the sparsely-populated event for the two previous years remained absent as the sun travelled with the Grand Prix circus across the Iberian Peninsula and to the small town south of Porto. The government subsidised meeting (Bellpuig was also financed by the Catalan 'Ajuntament') routinely provides the lowest attendance of the year but the track itself has a lot of character with its distinctive fine red soil and more fans than ever decided to attend the 2006 incarnation; they were rewarded with an epic.

Like a gazelle weaving and sprinting away from the hot pursuit of the single-minded leopard, so did Everts defend his racing line from the lust of Tortelli's twitching and ferocious KTM. It was a duel in every sense. Everts wasn't able to shred his second 'orange skin' and the gap between the pair never extended to beyond two seconds. In truth it looked like Tortelli had the upper-hand and was an entity of varying moves and desperation as Everts, smooth and unflinching as ever, defied the pressure and kept faultless. Tortelli managed one passing move but his brief tenure at the front lasted less than half a lap as Everts made a breathtaking counter-attacking manoeuvre to slip through a cambered right turn on which Tortelli had generously left a half-metre gap. The hunt began again.

Approaching the last circulation and sending backmarkers scurrying, a hand-wringing climax was scuppered when the Frenchman made a mistake on a steep step-up half a lap from the flag and crashed, injuring his foot. "Sebastien was there the whole race and pushing me," said Everts afterwards. "I had to ride defensively because I know he is very aggressive and could try anything. The moment he passed me I got him back going up the hill and I think that was an important move that decided the rest of the race."

If the riders were exhausted then the fans were also left fighting for breath. It was an exhilarating contest. Motocross and motorsport at it's finest.

The chance of a rematch was ruled out that same afternoon and indeed for the rest of the year when Tortelli went down early over the 'wave' section having been overtaken by Everts in the same spot were he was a victim two hours prior. A prostrate former World Champion was finally lifted to the medical centre where he was diagnosed with a dislocated hip. A return at the German Grand Prix two weeks later was dismissed with news that the luckless rider had broken knee ligaments and would need six months away from the sport. With a two year contract that would take him back to the US for 2007 it was a painfully short return for Tortelli to European shores.

His race status in the second moto was taken by Barragan and Strijbos who both earned overall podiums; a career first for a beaming Barragan. The Spaniard trailed Everts for the second bout but in truth the Belgian was riding nothing like at the level witnessed earlier. A third triumph took his career total up to 90 and for the first time whispers of reaching the magical 100 mark in his final season began to circulate with intent.

The MX2 class again dropped into the clutches of Rattray. The South African owned his second moto of the year after catching a pacey Rui Goncalves who was proving to be a fast starter on the Silver Action KTM and in front of his home fans. An electrical problem cruelly robbed him of a debut top three result but he had definitely caught the eye after also running with the leaders in Spain.

Philippaerts suffered machine trouble and the Italian did not disguise his frustration in the pit lane after two non-existent rounds, while Gundersen was sick. Cairoli unbelievably made the podium despite finishing in tenth position in moto two after becoming entangled in a first corner pile-up. It was the first piece of 2006 silverware for the friendly and outgoing Sicilian who was the fastest in the day's opening battle. The rider to watch though was Pourcel. The French youngster who was already catching unfair and lazy comparisons to Jean-Michel Bayle was again proactive and growing in stature. His small and thin frame yielded a confident and natural ability on the motorcycle and his double haul of runner-up positions placed him right behind a concerned Rattray.

R04 May 6/7 **Teutschenthal**

The first Grand Prix without the presence of Tortelli, Pichon and Coppins meant that the focus fell squarely on the next generation of the MX1 class to see who could attempt to overthrow Everts. After shining at Bellpuig, Strijbos, Leok and Barragan, all twenty years of age, emerged as the most suitable candidates and, although their best efforts were appreciated and not too far off the mark, Everts' second double of the season would be the start of a terrifying grip on the Championship that would slightly waver from time to time but never truly slip over the course of the next three months.

The pleasant May weather wafted in the

throes of summer as the techni-colour yellow fields rolled around the rural setting outside the city of Halle baring so many marks still of a dark pre-unification era. The World Championship had survived spring's tendency to produce a wash-out on its visits to Belgium, Spain and Portugal and while a large crowd basked in the generosity of the sunshine the

conditions again meant a tough physical test for the riders.

The Talkessel track flows. In fact its historic layout with cambered sweeping turns, dips, climbs and undulations is one of the more spectacular natural courses on the calendar. It is also quick. The emphasis on corner speed and with straights-a-plenty in between gave the sensation of a brutally fast prospect. This characteristic of Talkessel has its fans and critics within the riding fraternity but there is little doubt that the track can bite back if not given adequate respect. Big crashes for Pichon, Andrea Bartolini and Marc de Reuver in the last few years testify to this. In the 2006 edition Antonio Cairoli trundled back to his team after a heavy get-off in warm-up that left the Italian with a sore back and neck while in the MX1 morning

session a huge spill for Stephen Sword on the works Kawasaki saw the Scot out for the rest of the season with a complex break to his lower right leg.

The motos themselves had Everts prove that 'stalk' is cheap. The Belgian was so authoritative – a vein of form he would exercise to new heights in Japan two weeks later – that the sight of the 33 year old ploughing a course at the front would become one of the defining images of the season. While the German GP looked simple it was by no means a cinch. Strijbos and Cedric Melotte gave close company in the first moto while Leok fulfilled the position of a Yamaha wingman later in the day. Running with Everts did not look impossible, but from Germany onwards trying to actually pass the man was another feat altogether.

Needless to say the KTM team were decimated; their hopes of MX1 success crushed even before the fourth round but Barragan's continuing level of speed was cause for optimism and his relegation of Melotte for third spot in Moto1 had the Belgian Yamaha rider slapping the air in frustration.

The MX2 contest was all about Christophe Pourcel who peeled a leaf from the 'Everts manual' and followed the script thoroughly. The young Frenchman won his first Grand Prix with two absolute performances on a Kawasaki that skimmed the German mud like a rocket. With Cairoli lagging, Philippaerts off-key at the race where he earned his works KTM twelve months prior and Rattray falling to fourth in Moto1, Pourcel only had to worry about the surprisingly consistent De Reuver, although in truth the curves of Talkessel were all his. The Teutonic triumph would be an important step in the teenager's season. The confidence surge would be identifiable over the following rounds and he would leave Germany without the red plate for the last time.

The normally spacious paddock had to contend with the large influx of female racers for the first round of the Women's World Cup that was both a source of fascination and minor distraction for the GP boys. The opening race of a two-round series dominated by the trio of Katherine Prumm (New Zealand, Kawasaki), Livia Lancelot (France, Yamaha) and Stephanie Laier (Germany, KTM) delivered the best moto of the day as all three circulated close together until the flag and were separated by just over a second at the line. Prumm would gain the overall and the girls would visit again in Sweden.

R05 Sugo
Grand Prix of Japan

"Japan was special. As a rider you do not have many races like that, maybe once or twice in five or ten years. I was in another league that day and rarely is a Grand Prix so easy. I was having trouble concentrating in the first moto because my body was saying 'you don't need to push anymore' and it was tempting to ease off but it is wrong to think that way." Stefan Everts took his third win from three races in Japan over the course of the last eleven years and his post-GP words say it all.

The Yamaha owned Sugo circuit was back on the calendar for the second year in succession and enthusiastically received by most of the skeletal World Championship paddock once the jet-lag had subsided. The catchphrase surrounding the excellent 2005 edition with its detailed organisation, enthusiasm and fantastic track (loamy, lines, technical, big jumps) was 'why do we have to come all this way to find something so good?' and the same feeling was applied to the second expedition to the facility only a few kilometres from the road racing complex. The rough edges had been smoothed, the track altered and refreshed, more awareness led to more pubic and the Grand Prix still had the hallmarks of an annual World Championship event with Samurai warriors enacting a vibrant opening ceremony and enlarged media interest.

The make-shift paddock and diminished entry-list were clear signs that the orient adventure is a stretch too far for the privately-owned teams despite a travel subsidy for the top 15 riders in each series. The numbers were made up by a healthy quota of Japanese hopefuls, among them former GP rider Yoshitaka Atsuta who relished the chance to make old acquaintances. With the manufacturers towing their rigs to the detached second lower level of the paddock there was more of a chance to hide the latest technical innovations from the prying and crafty European lenses. Yamaha, Honda and Suzuki were all experimenting with electronic fuel injection while Suzuki had a new frame with revised bracing on the special machine of Shinichi Kaga. Not to be out-done KTM were using a second chamber on Carl Nunn's Akrapovic exhaust in MX2, said to lower the decibels and boost a little of the bottom range.

It was a great Grand Prix again for Yamaha with the two same winners from 2005 producing the goods once more. Everts was master of the dojo in MX1 and gave a preview of his speed with a comfortable pole position on Saturday in incredibly humid conditions. Friday had seen rain and – more worryingly – a thick fog obscure the circuit but the sun belatedly arrived from its good work over Europe to gently fry the soft mud for both days of action.

How and why was Everts so good? True, three of the participants from the electric multi-rider scrap in 2005 were missing, but the World Champion just seemed to have the technical course dialled quicker and better than anyone else. With a brace of decent starts any sense of drama was removed and the MX1 motos seemed to take longer than usual to reach their conclusion. One rider to cause a ripple was Ken De Dycker, flying solo in the CAS Honda squad. The lanky Belgian was by now fashioning a decisive manner of coming through the pack on the works spec CRF but was persistently cursed with the kind of starts befitting a production bike; he couldn't buy a holeshot. Even so he was particularly sharp at Sugo and his maiden GP podium completed an all-Belgian top three with Ramon earning the other slot to the satisfaction of Suzuki bosses.

Billy Mackenzie was both the aggressor and the defender as he blazed the first MX2 moto and then had to defend a third position from a determined Gareth Swanepoel. He also showed Pourcel the fastest lines in the opening foray. His repeat win at Sugo was something that no British rider had managed since Jamie Dobb in 2001 on a 125cc machine in Spain and certainly caught the attention of the Japanese and smiling Yamaha top brass. Bad news lay around the corner for Tyla Rattray, the fourth corner in fact of the second moto. A collision with Sebastien Pourcel put the South African on the ground. A suspected dislocated shoulder was later put down to a sprain and for the first time since 2002 a Frenchman was leading the MX2 World Championship as Pourcel took fourth. Cairoli surged ahead in Moto2 but was missing the consistency of De Reuver and Pourcel who were now clocking up the points.

At night the neon and cleanliness of nearby Sendai city captivated the riders and personnel spread around the hotels in the centre, and the camaraderie of travelling and racing so far from Europe was one of the genuinely enjoyable parts of the Grand Prix.

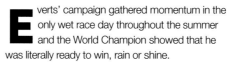

R06 Sevlievo

Grand Prix of Bulgaria

Everts' campaign gathered momentum in the only wet race day throughout the summer and the World Champion showed that he was literally ready to win, rain or shine.

After a stuffy and humid opening set of motos in both classes the second and final MX1 sprint caught the full brunt of a cloud-burst over eastern Bulgaria; the water dropped with such intensity that the track could no longer absorb the torrent and the mud shimmered with puddles that Everts would part like a Yamaha-mounted Moses on his way to a another double. "I normally enjoy playing in the mud but from the moment I felt the water getting inside my boots that was too much!" he offered.

Everts won the two motos again this time from an active Kevin Strijbos who gave his countryman a fair dose of pressure without really causing any hassle. "In the second moto the rain came and I had to ditch my goggles. I almost had to stop a few times and clear my eyes because following people was very difficult. There was so much water," said a blood shot Steve Ramon who, along with Strijbos, gave Suzuki the first of several double podium appearances. Jonathan Barragan did not last long in Moto2 with a sore knee and a headache courtesy of a fast dismount in the waves section proving too painful.

In a country that is still very much finding its feet economically and socially it was something of an eye-opener once again to travel to Sevlievo and find the best motocross facilities bar none on the World Championship calendar. The excellent infrastructure that had welcomed the series in 2002 and 2003 was not only still in place but had been improved and kept up to a fantastic standard. From the levelled, floodlit paddock to the timing towers, grandstands, parking and washing amenities the circuit gave the Grand Prix an instantly impressive edge and shouted '21st century top flight motocross'. With a well-attended music concert on Saturday night, an opening ceremony and flyover on Sunday the event was a proud and slick display and a fitting symbol of what can be achieved when motocross receives the support and backing of the government.

The race was sign-posted as far away as the capital of Sofia, some 130 miles. Hardly any of the riders stayed in campers and several teams even left their rigs at home due to the distance from western or central European bases but the importance of having a quality meeting like the Bulgarian Grand Prix on the calendar is as clear-cut to the sport as it is to the country itself in terms of the status in staging a World Championship motor sport event.

What the GP did lack was a sizeable crowd but there were more spectators than on the previous two visits and the ticket entry price of just 5 euros for the weekend seemed incredible but was relative. The track, with its heavily angled and long hill-side drags, was heavy on the throttle and the dry and packed soil became quite slippery when watered in an effort to contain dust.

Incredibly Marc de Reuver earned only his second career victory and his first moto win of the year with 25 points in Moto2. The likeable and charismatic Dutchman has not finished a full World Championship since 2001 due to a wretched spell of injuries to his head, hip, back and knee but now pushed himself firmly into MX2 contention. His triumph looked extremely unlikely on Sunday morning after a qualification heat prang had left him down in 25th on the gate for the motos. Victory from a similar position is unlikely to be seen again for quite a while. Having been shifted from the Dutch Champ KTM wing of the factory set-up to Georges Jobe's spacious MX1 awning David Philippaerts was suddenly back on the pace and not being shy with criticism of his former crew.

Pourcel, having taken the lead in the standings and finishing ahead of a weakened Rattray, was firmly into a mature 'title mode' where points definitely meant prizes. Surprisingly he was caught by both De Reuver and Rattray in Moto2 and had played second fiddle to Cairoli earlier in the day. Cairoli was a 'crashee' in the mud and not for the first or the last time in the season would see a good moto's work submerged by an incident in the other. De Reuver's achievement pulled him to within two points of Pourcel in the standings and he was easily the rider on a roll. Billy Mackenzie sank back into mid-pack only two weeks after ruling the competition at Japan but the British rider was competing with a broken left hand.

The sixth round of the Championship kicked off a busy three-week-three-race phase of the schedule that most of the riders were citing as the pivotal period of the season. In the case of Everts he was fortifying his castle with bigger bricks. De Reuver was now the main KTM threat to Pourcel, but all would change in the space of seven days.

June 10/11

R07 Montevarchi

R07 Montevarchi

Grand Prix of Italy

As per usual with the Italian round of the World Championship the venue changed for another year. The annual circulation among a small selection of the circuits in the country was this time widened to encompass the frankly unfit but wonderfully scenic Montevarchi, a short dash south of Florence.

The Grand Prix paddock last threaded their way up the narrow, steep and winding road to the facility in 2003 and the growth of the FIM series in that short time meant that Montevarchi was simply not well-equipped to handle the rows of Semis and hoards of fans. Happily the World Championships has left small and unsuitable circuits like Montevarchi behind so the 2006 edition of the Italian race was not particularly comfortable. The track itself was a strange entity. Hard-pack of course but tight and twisty with many turns folding back on themselves and the speed still quite high despite the 'Karting nature' of the layout. The high, angled climb out of the gate to the first turn would leave the slower starters with a lot of work.

Montevarchi was teeming with fans on Sunday – it seemed easier to beat Stefan Everts over two motos than find a parking spot near the track - and the Italian teams had gone to great lengths with their hospitality set-ups. Martin Honda in particular had a swarm of leggy models and VIPs hovering around their superb unit (year upon year the best in the paddock). The special visitors included MotoGP star Marco Melandri

and 250cc World Championship road racer Andrea Dovizioso. Antoine Meo was back on the Honda CRF 250R despite a broken knee ligament. The Frenchman was on the entry list mainly to give extra publicity to an adventurous fuel injection system on the 250. The project garnered its fair share of attention but ultimately failed at the first hurdle when it wrecked the engine during practice.

The MX2 class stole the show from the MX1 contest that had already become a one-man attraction. David Philippaerts announced his return as a protagonist in emphatic style with his first overall of the season and his dispute with Antonio Cairoli in the first moto was a more cut-and-thrust and less elegant version of the Everts-Tortelli extravaganza from Portugal; and just as gripping. The pair were split by just under a second at the finish and the rousing bellow of appreciation from the public, wedged into the small viewing areas, was tangible. The second race was even easier to chart and had more depth as a spectacle. Philippaerts' speed at the front from the first lap was almost as hot as the weather. However the 22 year old slid out before he could begin to pound the lap-times with regularity and handed the moto to a trio of Rattray, Rui Goncalves and Cairoli. Rattray was too hasty in seizing the lead from fellow KTM rider Goncalves and crashed, hurting his right ankle in the spill. The injury would haunt the South African over the coming weeks and ultimately wreck his title plight. Cairoli took over but was still not comfortable with his weak wrist and the crowd were captivated by a snorting and bucking Philippaerts, all strength and aggression and wielding the 250cc KTM like an 80. He was soon back in control of the Grand Prix and was marginally more cautious when ahead.

Ricci Racing rider Davide Guarneri had a noticeably raucous fan club in the small grandstand but he also unfortunately steered the noisiest bike with another silencer problem during the qualification heat that he had been leading. The Italian had to be disqualified in Bulgaria and nervous officials apprehensively approached the Ricci crew again to convey the bad news and that their man had to enter the Last Chance session. Marc de Reuver probably wished for a time penalty as it would make his two results on Sunday – in horrifically stark contrast to his accomplishment the week beforehand – slightly more acceptable and understandable. Sebastien Pourcel popped up in the top three in the first moto and Spaniard Carlos Campano clocked a career best with 8th in the second outing.

On the dry terrain where he had won motos in 125 and MXGP (the forerunner to MX1) in 2003 to initiate a second half season of supreme dominance Everts gave a repeat performance in MX1. After an unsurprising win ahead of Strijbos and Ken De Dycker for the opening race, the second MX1 moto delivered an interesting development and this time it was not down to freak weather as in Bulgaria. Strijbos was glued to Everts heels' when the growl from the works Yamaha morphed into an ear-endangering rasp. Closer examination of the right side of the YZ 450 going through the wave section revealed a cracked silencer at the end of the main tubing that was now melting a hole in the side panel. The race suddenly had a sense of drama as the implications for Everts' ailment could have swung the Grand Prix into Strijbos' favour. The Belgian's destiny and hopes for 2006 glory edged one step further to a positive conclusion though as he rode his luck and also rode through the problem. Amazingly he started to leave Strijbos behind. The bike looked as though it was lacking a little power on some of the uphills but it clearly wasn't impeding the World Champion and after a handful of laps the tension eased as it transpired that the silencer would not detach itself Guarneri-style. Another Grand Prix double was promptly confirmed but it was curious that Everts' machine was swiftly placed on the podium without any kind of sound check.

Seven rounds from seven also stretched his career tally to ninety-four and eleven motos in a row; a streak of results and level of confidence that was threatening to run away. After Italy he could afford not to finish three motos and still be at the top of the points table. "I don't get bored with winning because every race is a hard job! Kevin did well today to put some pressure on me, especially in the second moto," he remarked. "He is keeping me focussed lately and I have to keep pushing to stay in front." Extreme weather and a touch of mechanical difficulty had failed to prevent Everts from doing his job in the past week and now he was seven days away from coming through the toughest part of the season with an untouchable aura.

June 17/18

R08 **Matterley Basin**

R08 Matterley Basin

Fox British Grand Prix

The anticipated Fox British Grand Prix drew a bottom-heavy first half of the World Championship to a close as a weary paddock pulled into the brand new facility near England's south coast. The third event in the space of just over two weeks was again adorned with high temperatures and generous sunshine as the sustained pan-European heat wave stretched right across to a normally unreliable United Kingdom. A heightened sense of curiosity pervaded the Grand Prix community with the visit to the only unseen circuit on the World Championship schedule, while Youthstream approached the meeting with an extra observant eye and degree of trepidation as the race represented a 'dry-run' for the series promoter's crown-jewel event, the Motocross of Nations, later in the year.

The setting for the British round was quite magnificent. The track lay sprawled in the centre

of the deceptively steep 'dip' and lapped up against both sides of the gully like an eager tide. With all the hassle involved with not only running a 'meet' of that size but also creating a fresh circuit it was no surprise to see a few teething problems when it came to matters of organisation and logistics. The Grand Prix lacked a professional sheen that other established venues and clubs boast after years of experience. Still, for a first effort it was not too bad and had a major advantage with the geographical lie, affording almost 100% views of the action and enough space to be able to accommodate twice the quantity of fans that bothered to leave the saturation of the World Cup

and travel down the motorway.

The track was a victim of refused permanent planning permission and gave the appearance of being quite simplistic and very quick, but with the steady hand of Johnny Douglas Hamilton looking after the curves and gradients the natural ground gave opportunity for numerous step-ups and other little indentions. The riders were divided in their opinions and the terrain was the main cause. A lack of water meant that it was very dusty and a powdery top soil hid a hard and flinty surface underneath. Comments ranged from 'schoolboy track' and 'slippery mess' to general approval in quarters, no less from the MX1 World Champion himself who had to work a little harder for his food on this occasion and secure another double win bonus.

The British Grand Prix has routinely been among the best attended races since the event came back onto the calendar in 2004 after a three year hiatus. The atmosphere and roars of the ever-enthusiastic local throng floated up the hill on the Isle of Wight in '04 and echoed off the trees for a seismic din at Matchams Park twelve months earlier. The Basin dispersed the crowd around the huge expanses and slopes. It meant that the atmosphere wasn't quite as contained but the expectation and siren of the hundreds of air-horns still managed to send a ripple down the spine.

Whether you call it pressure or home advantage there was no doubt that the Brits were placed on a slightly different platform to the rest of the riders. The attention was homed onto MX2, and Billy Mackenzie wandered in from two accident-packed meetings in Bulgaria and Italy to get the flags waving in the first moto. The Scot was powerless to catch Philippaerts, again a pace-setter, and was hunted by Christophe Pourcel despite the will of 20,000-odd onlookers with two laps to go for the runner-up spot. Cairoli had started poorly and finished 6th while Rattray was unable to take his tender foot off the pegs around the right-hand corners and struggled to 17th and 15th. De Reuver hated the track and his season promptly went off the rails with 25th and 17th; rarely has a works KTM looked so slow. Mackenzie saw all hope of an overall home podium vanish when he ran off course in Moto2 and couldn't rise above 8th. The onus fell onto

seventeen-year old Tommy Searle whose argument with Sebastien Pourcel for third spot went into a last lap showdown. The Frenchman held the position starting the final circulation but the impressive Searle, in only his tenth World Championship race, retaliated and his successful manoeuvre instigated a very loud football-style cheer and brought Matterley Basin to its feet. The teenager was mobbed at the finish line in celebration of his first ever podium finish. Cairoli meanwhile had taken the initiative away from Philippaerts in the second race and the KTM rider sat behind in second, content in the fact that he had victory number two in the space of seven days.

MX1 witnessed the return of Josh Coppins and further weight and ammunition for the 'supporting cast' in their relentless but fruitless attempts to knock Everts from his fortress wall. In truth the New Zealander did not have anything like the condition or race-speed to place himself in the frame for the win but his podium was deserved and pleasing to see after his rotten luck in Belgium.

Everts made little contest of the first race. De Dycker and Coppins slugged out second position and some untoward tactics by the Belgian against his senior team-mate involved some brake-testing and blocking that verged very close to the line of being dirty. More of the same was seen in the second race as Strijbos pushed the CAS rider to the limit. Moto2 provided something of a novelty as Stefan Everts crashed. The slip happened on the fifth lap and dumped him from first to fourth. It was like hanging an even fatter carrot in front of the donkey. The more cynical might have believed that he had even done it on purpose! For another eight circulations the contents of Matterley Basin were entertained as '72' studied and eventually dispensed of Leok, Strijbos and Ramon for consecutive moto win thirteen.

Everts and Pourcel had come through the busiest section of the World Championship with results of 1-1-1 and 3-3-6 respectively and heading the standings of each class. There was palpable relief at the end of the afternoon as the intensity of Grand Prix motocross had finally relented. Round nine would not occur for another two weeks and the break was appreciated before the trip to Sweden. Matterley meanwhile had embraced an uneasy baptism and had less than three months to get ready for the Nations.

July 1/2

R09 **Uddevalla**

R09 Uddevalla

Grand Prix of Sweden

The fresh and breezy environment of Uddevalla, all trees, nature and long Swedish light, also ritually permeates the World Championship motocross gathering. The fixture is one of the staple elements of the schedule and has been every season without fail since 2001. Sweden formed a slice of the first FIM motocross competition and now, forty-nine years on, is still a reliable and awaited stop. The energy and enthusiasm of the club extends through the normally faultless organisation and willingness of the fans; all despite the fact that the Swedes have not produced a leading rider this century and still retain rosy memories of Peter Johansson's efforts in the old 500cc category.

The many virtues that Uddevalla enjoys as a venue (ample hard-standing space, good traffic access, close to a large town) had been tempered in recent years with a tired track. Verging on hard-pack in places the terrain was especially treacherous in the wet and the course's layout usually did not facilitate decent racing due to its tendency to flow into one line. The club took radical action for 2006 and not only reversed the track but added several new jumps and sections, including an interesting cambered penultimate turn before the finish line. Word of the re-sculpture wholeheartedly captured the attention of the paddock and the Swedish public it would seem as the circuit appeared much busier compared to recent

seasons. The alterations worked and the novelty of the new Uddevalla ensured that the lofty status of the Grand Prix of Sweden remained very much intact. The positive vibes about the meeting were further honed by a belting first MX2 moto.

Antonio Cairoli and David Philippaerts re-enacted their Italian Grand Prix spat to the delight of the multitudes condensed around the high rocky hillside flanking the circuit like a tidal wave waiting to break. The testy dice went down to a controversial climax. Taking different lines on the penultimate curve leader Cairoli seemed to have the win as he held the inside route into a dip and then a 45 degree right hand corner heading into a table top finish. Philippaerts then provided a suitable visualisation of his whole racing 'being'. His determination and win-or-crash mentality – normally evident in his free and ruthless riding style – meant that the race was not over. He threw the KTM on the outside of the dip and gunned the 250 on a much wider and faster outside line of the right-hander, promptly careering straight into the fence. Cairoli completed the jump and sailed past the chequered flag with his fist in the air. Philippaerts steered back on course and headed back to the podium for second place only to be told that he was in fact that winner having cut the timing beam situated at the bottom of the jump take-off first with his front wheel, even though Cairoli had owned the flag. The decision did not sit well with the World Champion. "On the last corner he went

very fast on the outside and won by less than a second," he commented. "I thought I had the race because he went crazy and straight on into the green fence. I don't think it was correct but Philippaerts is a very strong and fast guy."

It was the closest finish of the season and set a high standard for the rest of the Grand Prix. The second MX2 sprint could not match the former hysterics and Christophe Pourcel had enough of watching the Italians ahead of him. He escaped with the moto – only his third win of the year – ahead of Philippaerts (safe again with the overall) and the continually-impressive Tommy Searle (proving that Great Britain was no fluke) while Cairoli departed from his Yamaha three times for a disappointing end to the day.

Stefan Everts clearly liked the role of 'hunter' rather than 'hunted' as the second MX1 moto passed in similar style to the British affair. Victory had come without drama earlier in Moto1 in front of a strong Barragan probing the Scandinavian soil with an improved clutch on the KTM that gave the youngster his first ever MX1 holeshot. The second race was another thorough Everts exposition with a mistake coming on the first lap and then Belgian taking the entire moto to close a large time distance to Ramon at the front. To the pleasure of the public and onlookers who were getting decent value for their Krona, the undisputed class leader moved through to his habitual position on the last lap and left the rest of the MX1 field wondering just how the man could be beaten. Suzuki in particular seemed especially perplexed – although not totally unsurprised – as to how their rider didn't win. Josh Coppins debunked Strijbos into third overall while Gordon Crockard wandered in from the cold brought on by two years of injury with a partial-career-vitalising fourth position in the second heat.

With Sweden's famed reputation for attractive young ladies coupled with the second round of the Women's World Cup it is a wonder that the mostly sub-25 year old male contingency of the MX1 and MX2 classes actually got any work done. Livia Lancelot will look back on the first moto with a shiver as a crash while leading less than half a lap from the flag gave advantage to Katherine Prumm – still nursing a broken wrist – who would go on to be the second ever female World Champ.

July 15/16

R10 Sun City

R10 Sun City

Grand Prix of South Africa

The goggle incident of 2004 and the last lap crash of 2005 were finally laid to rest when Stefan Everts added the African continent to his vast geographical list of conquered soil. Another double moto success was a long overdue spoil for the Belgian who was sanctioned over his on-track spat with Mickael Pichon two years ago and then took his left hand off the bars to wave at the crowd while leading on the final circulation of the 2005 edition and promptly fell off gifting the win to Josh Coppins.

Everts was by now riding the equivalent of a runaway train of form, confidence and inevitability. The races were counting down and the mathematics being calculated towards a possibly historic and apt day of glory at Namur in three weeks time.

South Africa was a long stage of a marvellous trek that was entering its final phases for Everts; incredibly it was only round ten but the fact that he departed dominant again from an event that had been such an adverse experience for him in the past was further indication that 2006 was a walk of fate as much as being a walk in the park.

As with Sweden the MX2 class firmly stole the show and David Philippaerts was at the heart of the theft. Like or dislike the Italian there is little doubting the Latin temperate and fire to win explicit in his animated approach and the obstacle for his desire on this occasion was Tyla Rattray, himself a little psyched to make a splash at a race where he was the star.

The platform on which they entertained had been improved over the hard and rocky surface from the previous two Grand Prix. The entirely

man-made layout, located on a piece of land adjacent to the vast public car park at Sun City, was once again interesting and spectacular with its timing sections, big jumps and sandy stretch.

Designer Johnny Douglas Hamilton, working with Youthstream official Greg Atkins were able to count on almost ten times more material compared to the year before to mix in and soften the clay-ish dirt as well as a South African crew now gaining experience in the tendencies and demands of a changing motocross circuit.

Philippaerts and Rattray, already at odds over the former's controversial defection to the MX1 side of the KTM set-up, bashed each other repeatedly in a fraught contest for the opening MX2 moto. Philippaerts seemed to be the main instigator and his rattling tactics against the home favourite appeared to work as Rattray tried to come-back at his KTM adversary on the last lap but the 22 year old wasn't budging. "He saw that I was behind him and started doing some strange things like brake-checking me," commented Rattray. "I decided that the best option was to pass him but in the rhythm section he jumped onto me. We had a gap over Toni in third and we were racing for the win so it did not make much sense to be doing things like that and putting two KTMs on the ground."

"I was quicker in some parts of the track and he was better in others," countered Philippaerts who took his fifth win from the last eight motos. "We came close with some of our lines but I did not touch him."

If Philippaerts was unrighteous then his justice would be served in the second race when a crash trying to get past Billy Mackenzie led to a

damaged rear wheel that finally crunched half a dozen laps later. The DNF would be the first time he had dropped out of a moto top three for the past five Grand Prix and scuppered his valiant title charge somewhat. Carl Nunn was the surprise of Moto2 and led the initial half before being relegated by Cairoli and then Rattray; the Sicilian would earn his first overall victory of the season while Nunn enjoyed his maiden 2006 visit to the podium after nailing two excellent starts on the 250 SX-F. Marc de Reuver was nowhere to be seen again and did not score points in either heat for his lowest moment of the year while Pourcel also struggled. His tenth position in Moto1 after a spill trying to move into fifth was his worst finish of an otherwise proficient term so far.

The South African Motocross Grand Prix was a first class event in practically every way. The hospitable and welcoming hosts at the leisure and hotel complex of Sun City – sadly rumoured to be entertaining for the last time after three years in charge as the race is provisionally slated to move south to Durban in 2007 – had placed care in the details such as the presentation of the different areas of the circuit and track (good commercial presence, slick organisation). Despite the shrinking presence of the grandstands the few that were employed for 2006 were full and gave the impression of a busy meeting.

MX1 saw the same top three of Everts, Coppins and Ramon setting the pace and the trio were becoming consistent 'podiumees' entering the last third of the campaign. The only drama lay in the at-times-perilous trawl past some of the backmarkers; local riders entered to flesh out a slim entry list and woefully incapable of running at an acceptable Grand Prix speed. Everts survived the ordeal but some were not so lucky. Set to collect a position inside the top ten Javier Garcia Vico had his line blocked over a double by a lapper and the huge crash saw the Spaniard concussed and taken to hospital. Apparently his bed was unknowingly placed next to his careless competitor in the ward for an extra little bit of salt-rubbing.

Everts probably had more attention than usual on his last circulation in the second moto. "I was taking it easy on the jumps and making sure that I did not do anything stupid. At one point I thought 'shall I wave again?' but in the end I wasn't tempted to play with fate!" he said. Indeed…

R11 July 29/30 Loket

R11 Loket

Grand Prix of Czech Republic

The World Championship sped up a notch when the series arrived to Loket just outside the splendorous town of Karlovy Vary for round eleven; quite literally.

The end of the season was rapidly approaching with the Grand Prix of Belgium taking place one week later and the MX1 contest moving towards an obvious conclusion. The Czech circuit – like Teutschenthal – was a fast and throttle-cable-shredding layout, draped across a steep hill deep in the west of the country like a soggy blanket. The track encompassed a variation of cambered turns, drops and climbs with surprisingly few jumps within close public proximity although retained a natural and earthy feel that no doubt warmed the cockles of the older riding element. Traction was a problem as rubber scratched a hard and stony dirt that was again mainly dry throughout the weekend as the Grand Prix circus continued its love affair with the sunshine. Some ferocious showers paid a visit on Saturday evening but the temperatures ensured that the track was dusty rather than dirty.

Stefan Everts was drawing nearer to his goal. The fact that he had already celebrated two World Championships at Loket (2002 and 2003) was not lost on the Belgian who calmly went about his business and verbalised his mantra of 'taking each weekend and each race at a time' in front of an enquiring media collective curious as to the mounting pressure of another title. A tenth success at Loket would mean a fantastic setting and culmination for his achievements at his favourite track, Namur, seven days afterwards.

Timed Practice highlighted the state of play with six riders inside the same second and Kevin Strijbos sealed his debut pole position at the site of his maiden victory (and that of the RM-Z 450 Suzuki) in 2005. With the widest, flattest and longest start straight on the calendar housing the start gate, qualification lost a little of its importance and this was backed up by Everts' solitary three fast attempts in the 30 minute period. The stretch from the line ran into an initial hairpin uphill left corner that must rank as one of the toughest, being especially tight for 30 braking and aggressive riders.

The significant pile-up of the day came in MX2 Moto1 when Cairoli, Gundersen, Christophe Pourcel and Billy Mackenzie had to pick up their bikes. Pourcel and Cairoli came back reasonably convincingly. Gundersen and Mackenzie did not, in another Grand Prix where the Yamaha again didn't seem quite the fire-bred it used to be.

After his bad luck or penance in South Africa (whichever way you want to look at it) David Philippaerts became the most successful MX2 rider of the season with his fourth overall success at Loket and fourth win from the last five Grand Prix. The Italian gave motos to Rattray and Cairoli and yet again managed to rub someone up the wrong way. This time an exchange or three with Pourcel for second place in race two had the French teenager seething. "Philippaerts was aggressive and tried some dangerous moves. I did the same to him. If he wants to ride dirty I can do this too, there is no problem with that," he said. Pourcel earned the runner-up spot and a place in the top three next to his new nemesis, and Britain's Carl Nunn who was getting out of the gate as well as anyone and finessing his KTM in his laconic and smooth style was again a podium visitor. Marc de Reuver shook off his bizarre mid-season slump to lead both races at one stage but could not maintain the pace of his pursuers as Rattray went from elation to deflation when a sizeable crash in Moto2 bent the bars of the 250F into the shape and angle of a road-racing clip-on.

The track favoured a top five start for victory and permitted a blurring speed that allowed few chances for riders to make up ground through the pack. The MX1 and MX2 fields were quite dispersed and Rattray's hunt, play and despatch of De Reuver in the opening sprint was entirely watchable for his first 25-pointer since April. Everts' faced a similar hounding from Josh Coppins for a good two thirds of MX1 race one but however much the New Zealander tried to break the three bike lengths that separated him from a rare demotion of the Championship leader Everts did not fault nor drop his pace. Eventually Coppins had to concede but his 2006 spurs had been earned. No such distraction faced the Yamaha man in the second outing after he had overtaken Barragan and Strijbos in the early laps.

The Suzuki rider suffered with a loose clutch lever in the first race and was also pushed around by De Dycker. "I was pissed off," the 20 year old said after checking his 450 for red marks. "I went to see him and asked if he knew how to race. He said that it was part of racing but in my book that kind of stuff isn't. I don't really care about that thing with Kevin. He started it by brake-checking me on the slow hairpin so I don't know why he is mad," De Dycker levied. Strijbos despairingly had to watch elder countryman Everts drift past later in the afternoon and could not repeat his team-lifting exercise of twelve months earlier.

The Grand Prix ended like part one of a momentous '72' trilogy. The background and leg work of the story had been set-up and now the second part of the saga was ready. A special day awaited for Everts just one week later, and then the days and weeks to his retirement (embracing the sub-story of a remarkable 100 career victories, standing at a towering 98 after Loket) at Ernee would conclude an eighteen year existence as the sports' most decorated participant. Namur beckoned first…

August 5/6

R12 **Namur**

R12 Namur

Grand Prix of Belgium

Stefan Everts' inevitable tenth World Championship and sixth title in succession, the first rider ever to register so many in a row, deservingly dwarfed the Belgian Grand Prix. The results show that Everts eased to his twelfth win of the year and Antonio Cairoli captured his second MX2 triumph of 2006 but the weekend will be remembered only for the scenes that celebrated a rider, career and archetypal ambassador for motocross.

The MX1 podium ceremony with Josh Coppins and Steve Ramon was nominal, for the champagne, mass jubilation, video clips, commemorative plaque presentation, tears, embraces and clamour of the watching public that followed. 2006 Namur was a career-defining moment for number '72', who now had '10' and reached a GP tally of '99'.

The 'Citadelle' fortification, pre-dating 890AD, was a strategic site atop an enormous mount in the city centre with the Sambre and Meuse rivers curling around it. Within this historical location, long the venue of sieges, attack and defence (indeed the town was at various stages Spanish, Austrian, French or Dutch and was only demilitarised in 1977) motocross also had an important role and had witnessed its own battles through the grounds and racing up and down the vast hill since 1957.

At more than 2440 metres in length the narrow, fast and relatively jump-less track was almost twice as long as standard FIM regulations and this was just one of the concessions given to a Grand Prix that seems to formulate part of the essence of motocross racing.

Skipping under a bridge, through dense woodland and even over a road, the track forces a more 'enduro approach'. Some riders revelled in deviation from the norm and embraced the atmosphere of Namur while others remained unsure on the throttle, the near-vertical drops, the close proximity of the trees, the protruding roots, high speed and harsh contrasts between light and shade impeding visibility meant unnecessary extra danger. For the spectators – like the Isle of Man TT – the thrill of watching motocross transplanted from the confines of a purpose-built circuit to a more 'ordinary' setting provided a wonderful contrast and enforced admiration.

Although for all its virtues as an authentic test of rider and machine and a novel spectacle, Namur is neither a practical viewing experience nor a landscape for decent racing. Trudging to a far section normally means sacrificing half of a 40 minute moto. The track is not easy for overtaking and running off-line carries its own perils as

Namur-rookie Tommy Searle found out in his MX2 heat race when he clattered an oak and went to hospital with concussion. As a rule-of-thumb if a rider does not exit the flat parade ground (the 'Esplanade', accommodating the gate, pitlane, wave sections and a large leap into the park) in the top five then his chances of victory are extremely slim. The pack is normally well-stretched by the end of a frantic first lap.

For 2006, as is the usual custom for Namur, the teams were sheltering from the rain on Thursday and Friday. The weekend would be dry but the downpours helped soften the track so that by the end of practice on Saturday the terrain was incredibly rough and bumpy; hugely technical but also creating a journey a little more fraught for the MX1 and MX2 competitors. The wear and tear was elevated by the presence of the Veteran and Senior World Cups won by Marc Van Den Brink and Thierry Godfroid respectively.

Everts was assisted in part by Kevin Strijbos, his nearest and sole remaining threat, who threw himself hard into the steep step-ups scaling their way back to the Esplanade trying to avoid a toiling Cedric Melotte during practice. The Belgian took the brunt of the crash on the left side of his chest and was originally feared to have cracked several ribs.

With his seventh pole position of the season and his closest rival struggling to be fit, the solitary point that Everts required by 5pm on Sunday was by no means a stretch. The Belgian's previous nine titles in all classes were now returning to help him with an unflinching approach to a hectic weekend; the professional veneer was more strained but he generally handled a powerful glare from the customary spotlight. "I was either signing autographs or I closed the door to the camper, there was nothing in between."

Team-mate Cedric Melotte finally showed some of his mettle that had been obscured in '06 by a wrist injury, an energy sapping virus and even obscure incidents such as getting a stone trapped in his throat at Sun City and then a rock caught in his boot at Loket. The Belgian, born locally, who has such sweet memories of his first ever GP win (one of only two so far) from 2003 and a 650cc success, led the first moto from Everts. The Yamaha duo took turns to wear Acerbis' garish 2007 yellow kit. On Sunday it was Melotte's shift but the 'canary' could not head the flock for long as Everts wings beat faster. Once in front he began to separate himself from his pursuers as Coppins and Ramon also filtered through. Jonathan Barragan was a first lap victim

as the large jump off the Esplanade saw Josef Dobes land his Suzuki on the Spaniard's left shoulder and he departed to hospital for a painful check-up.

Everts raced the track and faced the trickiest conditions with bigger bumps and rougher ruts in Moto2 but was undeterred in another escape act. Coppins and Ramon followed diligently with Strijbos earning fifth overall behind Melotte. "The last laps came up and I started to think that the moment was arriving but I forced myself to wait and concentrate. When I came onto the Esplanade for the last time the tears broke out, I eased off the gas and the last few metres of that race were simply incredible," the World Champion commented.

The formulaic construction of MX1 was off-set by the bigger picture and MX2 once again unveiled its fair quota of drama. Moto1 held watchers attentive as leader David Philippaerts, who was bashing his way around the track with risky but effective persistence, finally ran into some green fencing and the material churned into his back wheel and chewed the back brake. Cairoli was in close company and inherited the number one spot for his eighth moto of the year which he increased to a total of nine with a softer outing in the second race. Philippaerts ditched his KTM twice in the first three laps and apparently flipped Billy Mackenzie – his tormentor in South Africa – the finger as the Scot came round on the next lap after the Yamaha man had to ramp the Italian in the immediate wake of his second hasty error.

Tyla Rattray had confirmed his participation in the 2007 MX2 series on Saturday but a slip at the start of the first outing left him more than half a lap behind and seventeenth position naturally dented his overall ranking. Despite a fall in Moto1 Christophe Pourcel slimmed the point damage to Cairoli by taking second overall from his brother Sebastien who actually remained on the 'island' for two races for his maiden 2006 podium. The younger French sibling now held a 26 point advantage from Cairoli with 150 left in the pot.

R13 Desertmartin

August 26/27

R13 Desertmartin

Grand Prix of Northern Ireland

The trip to Northern Ireland and a Grand Prix being run on a Sunday for a change was not to everybody's liking. At least for the group of protesters that gathered by the entrance to the Desertmartin facility on Sunday morning to voice their opposition to a herd of four-strokes blazing a racket across the tranquillity of the Sabbath.

The meeting had been switched from the normal Saturday fixture to maximise the potential of a late August bank holiday weekend and also use the chance to gain any extra exposure.

While the minority outside expressed their disgust, inside the splendidly confined and interesting elevations of the sandy Irish course the fans congregating in the narrow viewing enclosures were treated to the best MX1 Grand Prix of the year.

Desertmartin was the first of two sand tests within a week for the riders and at this late stage in the season the physical demands of both tracks were being eyed with apprehension. The feeling in the paddock was like many were 'sucking in their breath' and the community just didn't quite have the same buzz about it as usual. That the Grand Prix riders almost universally liked the technical aspects of the extremely rough dark terrain was token, but the end of a long season, with commitments both internationally and nationally for many, was drawing near and a little lethargy was beginning to creep in.

Stefan Everts certainly bemoaned the fact that his three week break from a diminishing World Championship career had been full of off-track duties and retirement preparations in the wake of his Namur coronation. For the first time in 2006 the Belgian seemed to reveal a shade of his thirty-three years and he would be frustrated in his impatience to celebrate win number 100. A strong gust on the hilly circuit meant that battleship grey clouds regularly paid a visit and after surveying the hard work of the riders on a track that got rougher by the lap dumped light showers and moved on.

The opening MX1 moto was a re-run of the first Czech Republic chase. This time Coppins hung onto the rear wheel of Everts for the entire forty minutes and the Yamaha rider was not quite the superlative figure he had been at the same venue (and Desertmartin's World Championship inauguration) in 2005. It was exciting viewing when the realisation sunk in that Coppins could actually match Everts' lap-times. Backmarkers did not help the New Zealander's cause but the old problem of actually trying to overtake Everts

was never more apparent. Coppins had tried a number of modifications in practice, including a different cylinder head, to get the Honda on the pace and his first pole position of the season was a small clue that the CAS team had produced some good work over the course of Saturday.

The second race was a revelation and incredibly was the first time that Everts had been beaten in a head-to-head scrap in 2006. Coppins was so pumped by his pursuit and insurgence that he seemed to almost be trembling in the press conference afterwards with the adrenaline and satisfaction of an accomplishment that looked as though it might not have been actually possible before the chequered flag at Ernee. After the 29 year old had taken the lead with a move that had the crowd cheering/gasping he pushed hard to deflect Everts' counter and entering the last five minutes the pair began to separate for the first time. It was apparent in the last two laps that Everts had eased off the gas and saw that his quietly-spoken aim of remain unbeaten to the climax of the season had been crushed. "In the second moto I wanted it more," Coppins admitted. "I was able to do some nice things on the bike that I normally cannot and which you usually see Stefan pulling-off first and I was happy, taking confidence from that. We have been discussing strategies on how to beat Stefan. One of those was to stick with him and look and learn, let him have a small gap and then come back at him. It worked quite well in the first moto but I was not able to make a pass. Normally I can make a good start but then Stefan picks up his pace and then disappears, so we wanted to try something different. I would say that this is one of the best GPs of my career."

"The track was hard and very demanding," lamented Everts, who was extremely gracious in the unfamiliar position of defeat. "The first race was exciting and in the second Josh was so fast. At one point I could not stay with him anymore and physically I was finished. I think that we had the same speed but he was a bit stronger. I have been maybe a bit too busy with other things since winning the Championship. We were doing some very fast things around the back of the track and for that you have to stay focussed. I am happy for Josh; he has been working hard for this."

Behind the two Ken De Dycker picked up his second podium of the season after a sizzling comeback ride from a second corner fall in the first moto. His flight was exhausting but dragged him up to third in the race. He would pay the

physical costs after lunch and lose another third spot to Barragan in a bizarre second outing that saw the tall Belgian greatly varying his pace and conceding a position to the Spaniard, attacking again and then giving up.

Strijbos sealed fourth despite a delicate groin and his ambition of the runner-up spot in the series was boosted by his team-mate's misery. Ramon's second moto crash after losing control through the whoops was particularly hard and the former 125 World Champion nursed a concussion and an injured hip. Strijbos' cushion in the points table had grown to forty with just one hundred left to win while Ramon was searching for another kind of comfort altogether. Gordon Crockard encouraged the home fans with a decent fifth position in the first moto despite crunching his left foot on the tricky whoops but a prang coming into the double-lined hairpin by the pits later on left the luckless Irishman off the leader-board in Moto2.

For once MX2 took a back seat to the fantastic entertainment offered by MX1, especially as Tyla Rattray's speed was superior and he ruled both motos in a spirit and fashion that Everts would have applauded and perhaps even rued after the Irish proceedings had closed. A spectacular first corner pile-up that saw Rui Goncalves flip over the fence into another part of the track and left also Gundersen, Caps and Searle on the ground got the trigger fingers clicking on the cameras. Dutchman Marc de Reuver was a favourite but had to stop behind a fallen David Philippaerts on the initial lap of Moto1 and the incident meant a forty minute climb through the field for both. De Reuver was unable to reel in Rattray in Moto2 once he had reached second position and instead had a boring race in front of Christophe Pourcel. The Kawasaki rider was unperturbed by the increasing pressure of the impending MX2 title conclusion and rode a sensible meeting to second overall, edging more points over Cairoli who had fallen out of third spot in Moto2 and had to be content with a recovery to seventh after earlier being runner-up behind Rattray.

A severely fatigued riding collective disbanded swiftly on Sunday with the penultimate Grand Prix of the year just a few days away.

September 2/3

R14 Lierop

R14 Lierop

Grand Prix of The Netherlands

" I started in 1989 and now we are in 2006, so that is eighteen years to try and win 100 GPs; it has been a long road. Counting from one to ten in terms of titles can take some time, but one to one hundred is something else." What also took a long time to count was the distance Stefan Everts finished ahead of Josh Coppins in both motos (well over one minute combined) through the Lierop sand that managed to out-rut, out-bump and out-rough even Desertmartin. The Dutch terrain was quite phenomenal and the six hours of drizzle on Sunday made the dark surface more sapping.

The carved and rippling course saw more than its fair share of crashes and the machines of MX1 and MX2 were worked hard in the conditions. The technical dimensions of the sand separated the capable from the incapable on the first laps and the races were among some of the more processional seen this season.

Everts was in his element and from his pole position on Saturday it was clear that he could not have wished for a better time to visit the site of 2005 title celebrations and a Motocross of Nations win in 2004 in a renewed bid for the 'ton'. "It is one of the nicest surfaces to ride because you can find some really nice timing sections and I love it. This is my playground," he said in an uncharitable mood.

Once more Coppins was the best of the rest and Steve Ramon defied hip pain to score his eighth podium from fourteen Grand Prix. Strijbos was right behind him and curiously mute with sixth and fourth after changing engines for a slightly stronger power delivery from his works Suzuki and then still not being wholly satisfied with his set-up come Sunday. An enlarged radiator on Strijbos' RM-Z was helping with cooling and various means of makeshift filters on side panelling and plastics were also visible through the paddock to cope with the throttle-straining sand.

Outside of Everts' authority - that was as impeccable as his Japanese Grand Prix conquest four months earlier - Jonathan Barragan was the pick of MX1. The Spaniard dumped the Iberian-stereotype-of-excellence-solely-on-hard-pack to come back from a blameless first corner crash to ninth and then take an impressive third in the second moto. Like many of the leading elite in both classes Barragan bases himself in Belgium and the hours

of practice on similar types of tracks had rubbed off. The 20 year old was looking more and more like a serious prospect for upset in 2007 and was losing his rough edges.

Brian Jorgensen was unable to resist tears several times in a genuinely heart-wrenching announcement of his retirement on Saturday evening. The Dane identified his win at Teutschenthal in 2004 as a career highlight and explained how the memory of his late father helped him achieve the surprising double moto success after missing the previous meeting with a wrist operation. Jorgensen's news came as no surprise in the wake of yet more injury woes in 2006 but his friendly and amusing demeanour would be missed. It also left Honda's rider roster for 2007 looking decidedly light. Javier Garcia Vico opted out of a hard Lierop test with a damaged left ankle and Coppins had already been swayed by Everts' enormous vacant boots at Yamaha.

Christophe Pourcel placed half of his beret on the MX2 World Championship with exceptionally controlled races to third and first for only his second victory of the year. His pace in the sand was quite surprising considering the famed proficiency of his rivals but the composed manner of this latest result was by now overly familiar after a campaign of consistency perfectly designed for title success. His steadiness was placed in contrast with the failures of specialists De Reuver and Philippaerts, both of whom dipped their KTMs into the sand. Philippaerts should have won the opening race but an inexplicably slow crash when his front wheel found a hole while being distracted by a yellow flag for a fallen backmarker dropped him to fourth. He then snapped and poked at the back of Pourcel in the final two laps for third but just when he had re-entered the top three on the final circulation another dismount knocked his stuffing wayward and meant a slot of eighth place. An early spill and trouble restarting his 250F in Moto2 instigated a trip back to the paddock and

the second lacklustre Grand Prix in a row from one of the more sensational if erratic performers in the '06 competition. De Reuver had the dampened enthusiasm of the crowd behind him but hit a wall in Moto1 and fell off in Moto2. "I am not a quitter and have never been but I couldn't even ride over those bumps. I felt ashamed that I could not give them what they deserved," the Dutchman admitted.

Antonio Cairoli inherited the spoils of Philippaerts' earlier misfortune to win his tenth moto of the season (four more than the next most successful rider, his luckless countryman) but the points he had nipped from Pourcel were lost after a poor start in Moto2 and he finished third, leaving the standings margin at a cheek-bellowing twenty-eight points with just fifty remaining. Rattray's sharpness was blunted by a set of starts less succinct than his Irish launches and although he closed down Pourcel with inevitability in the second moto his attack was not followed through as the Frenchman dropped his lap-times and left the burly South African looking the weaker. Full credit to Rui Goncalves for a fine fourth position overall and making the most of factory suspension his team had taken delivery of at Desertmartin.

Everts dropped his Yamaha upon finishing his 100th Grand Prix win in all categories and danced for joy. It was another priceless moment for the Belgian who in a matter of just two weeks would lay a remarkable career to rest in France.

September 16/17
R15 Ernée
Grand Prix of France

So to Ernée. The final Grand Prix and the last chapter of a 2006 season where a career would end and the victorious path of another would begin. Two riders split by fifteen years and 99 victories.

Stefan Everts's fourteenth win from fifteen permitted a points haul of 739 from a possible 750, saw 22 motos won consecutively, naturally meant a 100% podium record and produced a campaign with a lowest result of third place. After his domination at Lierop the French Grand Prix seemed like his giant boulder of form was nearing the bottom of the hill. Christophe Pourcel on the other hand finally succeeded in rolling his stone to the peak in MX2 and had the applause of his countrymen to crown the feat.

A very wet Friday meant a sodden track on Saturday and a reduced practice and qualification programme. Mickael Pichon, who had managed a handful of laps at Zolder and had not been seen since, was making his Grand Prix goodbye and took his 26th pole position in the last three years. Sebastien Pourcel was fastest in MX2 by a thousandth of a second for the closest chrono in recent memory.

The motos started on a rough track with plenty of ruts but Pichon's didn't find any of them. Josh Coppins closed his line unintentionally exiting the first corner and the former World Champion hit the floor hard sustaining a broken nose and a concussion. Being taken away on a stretcher it was hardly the parting wave he imagined.

Coppins would also fall in the same race, at least twice, and finish sixth for his worst moto finish since returning at Matterley Basin eight events ago. Everts meanwhile, bedecked in special white and gold Acerbis gear and a commemoratively painted Yamaha with a chequered flag design bearing the name and date of each of his 100 victories, set off on the first of his double moto wins (his 12th set of the year) the white Pirellis supporting a rider who barely took his feet off the pegs.

Strijbos had a lonely Grand Prix with third and fourth and was missing an edge of speed after spending more than a week practicing on the new 250cc Suzuki in prep for his MX2 role for Belgium at the Nations. Nevertheless his better starts, ahead of team-mate Ramon, confirmed the 21 year old's 2006 runner-up status in the Championship.

Jonathan Barragan should have taken his third podium in France until he stalled the KTM while in third place in the second moto and Leok moved past Strijbos for third as Coppins resumed his usual position in the trail of Everts. Leok book-ended his season with podiums and equalled his highest result with second overall; much to the pleasure of Kawasaki bosses gathered for Pourcel.

The teenager could not catch Cairoli in MX2 Moto1 but was raucously cheered by the crowd with every twitch and throw of the KX 250F as he pursued the Sicilian and eventually engaged in a fantastic squabble in the second sprint. A two lap flurry of lead changes induced roars equivalent to a passionate football derby and was easily the highlight of the day. Pourcel slipped ahead, needing just one point from the moto, but then forced a gasp from the multitudes as he crashed after hitting neutral and dropped back to fifth. The circuit held it breath as Pourcel finally managed to restart and then watched in disbelief as he surged after Philippaerts for third position and hassled the KTM rider, with whom he has already had some physical run-ins this season, until the last set of step-downs before the chequered flag. It was cocky, entertaining and wholly admirable. Pourcel doesn't speak much but manages to say a lot with his riding.

At eighteen years of age the adoration and clamour seemed a little overwhelming for Pourcel who can be described as reserved, or disinterested in the off-track distractions of being a motocross star at the best of times. That he deserved the World Championship was out of the question, that he was a popular choice as a number one and an ambassador for the MX2 series was questionable.

Toni Cairoli graciously handed over his number one plate, while further down the field Tyla Rattray was a sullen figure in the living area having watched his third position in the Championship been robbed by Philippaerts at the last possible moment. Two shocking starts meant that the South African was never going to trouble the leaders as the Italian spent the second moto being informed of Rattray's whereabouts, scoring two third positions for the runner-up spot overall and a top three berth – tied on four GP victories with Rattray for the season.

At the culmination of the second MX1 moto and his 27th moto success from 30 Everts went

for a half a victory lap with a large white flag stating 'That's all Folks!'…it was hard to imagine what more the 33 year old could have brought to motocross. Team Manager Michele Rinaldi offered a different perspective. 'He is going to stop his career while still winning races and this is something unbelievable because you do not see this often, in any sport not just motocross.' Rinaldi Team co-ordinator Mino Raspanti echoed a question that many may have thought at some stage. 'I understand why Stefan wants to stop, but it is still a bit surprising because he is winning all the time so why retire? Then again I suppose if he wants to finish his career as World Champion it's the best move.'

Everts did not reach the same pitch of emotion as Namur, but maybe it was asking too much for the Belgian to take everything in at once, something he hinted as himself in the midst of the post-race clamour. "I really wanted to enjoy this day and try to capture a lot of things that I can remember later about the weekend," he commented. "It has been a fantastic year and an awesome ride. Just before the second race I was getting emotional when the '15 second board' went up. It was a tricky moment. I said to myself for the last time I am going to go for it and enjoy it, and I did."

Somewhere among the fuss Brian Jorgensen also signed off his Grand Prix career and 2002 125cc World Champion Mickael Maschio declared the end of his riding days at 33 years of age on Saturday night.

And so the 2006 campaign wound to a halt. Outside of the Kawasaki and Yamaha camps the atmosphere was a little subdued. Many teams packed up quickly and made their exit from the circuit. The Grand Prix series had finished for another year but with the Nations just one week away there was still work to be done before tools could be downed.

September 23/24
Fox Motocross of Nations
Matterley Basin

Fox Motocross of Nations

Matterley Basin, England

The mammoth crowd that jammed Ernée in 2005 came as a partial shock to many who were expecting a good attendance but could not have imagined the numbers and sight of a 40,000 plus gathering packed into the French valley. It was a re-affirmation of the Motocross of Nations; a second birth if you will of a tournament that had gathered the three best riders from competing countries across the globe for the last sixty years.

The 60th edition of the annual contest took place at Matterley Basin and the spectator numbers swelled further to positively establish the event as the largest and most atmospheric meeting on the calendar.

There must have been over 50,000 people submerged into the bowl and draped in the colours of a generous quota of the 31 entered nationalities. The cosmopolitan element and the different format of the Nations (three riders, three categories – MX1, MX2 MX Open – three motos with each class racing the other, reversed points, five results from six registered and lowest total wins) gives the meeting that special flavour and constitutes the perfect way to close any kind of motorsport schedule.

Team USA were partially dented by Ricky Carmichael's shoulder injury. James Stewart (along with AMA Lites Champ Ryan Villopoto making his Nations debut) slipped into the MX1 slot and Carmichael's Suzuki team-mate Ivan Tedesco substituted. Tedesco himself had missed the AMA Outdoor season but carried vital experience from his maiden appearance and success in France the year before. America were still the strongest team and with at least half of their scores coming via top three results their seventeenth, and record triumph having overtaken Great Britain's total of sixteen, was forthcoming. The trio would defend their crown from Belgium and New Zealand with Italy just missing the podium by two points.

With the unprecedented quantity of spectators (Stefan Everts: "I think that was one of the biggest crowds at a motocross event I have seen; it was incredible") the site burgeoned. The facilities aimed at a turn-out not too dissimilar to the creditable flock that came to the British Grand Prix in June strained to cope. Security and containment seemed the worrying issues and there was an odd mixture of excitement, disbelief and panic on Saturday evening when the promoters saw the throng that day was already larger than most Grand Prix; and that was just for practice and qualification. It proved again that having the Americans as part of the show really

pays off. Rapid co-ordination was needed with the police to ensure grid-lock did not ensue Sunday evening but a large section of the camping fraternity – that must have accounted for at least half of the overall figures and filled numerous fields around the site – stayed pitched to carry on the party. The track had been modified in sections and generous rainfall on Friday and Sunday morning helped created a rough terrain the antithesis of the dusty and slippery surface three months before.

Team USA may have re-polished the Chamberlain trophy but their riders did not own a chequered flag in the three races. Instead Stefan Everts closed his career in '2006 fashion' by taking Motos 1 and 3 with another reliable and emphatic display made all the more obvious by his incomprehensible ease on the bike and vast chunks of lap time rooted to the pegs. Stewart had crashed in Moto1 (MX1 and MX2 together), ruling out a duel between the two high-profilers, but his confidence and determination on the bike oozed through an attention-grabbing natural talent and he closed down some twenty seconds and at least three positions to pass Villopoto for the runner-up place. The Lites number one introduced himself to Europe and confirmed his status as America's most exciting new star. The seventeen year old scooped overall honours in the MX2 class, and with finishes of 4th and 5th Suzuki's Steve Ramon was the best in MX Open.

If Everts was the undoubted winner on the day then he was upstaged only by fellow Yamaha rider Antonio Cairoli on his YZ 250F. The second moto (MX2 and MX Open) saw the fantastically flamboyant Sicilian exchange pleasantries with Townley and Villopoto over a flurry of laps and a pulse-racing spell of close racing and position-swapping that instantly defined the event and Motocross as a premier spectacle. His aggressive, 'American' style was delightful and bursting with confidence. Once into second and with his MX2 rivals two seconds adrift he then charged after Ivan Tedesco, who had been leading from the first corner, and was pushed on by the masses keen to see some US authority overthrown. Tedesco slowed on the 450 struggling a little with a lack of race time and Cairoli had a rare MX2 success at the Nations that normally (and naturally) favours the bigger machines. Ivan would crash deep into the 30 minutes and 2 laps – that seemed punchier and more practical than a drawn out 35 minute GP heat – and would go down again in the final sprint but his efforts of 6th and 9th was important to the final Yankee tally.

Josh Coppins had a spectacular superman

crash as he lost control going up the tricky wave section in the final moto of the day but his results of 6th and 8th coupled with Ben Townley's impressive return to European soil (5th and 3rd) gave the Kiwis a well-earned rostrum celebration.

The hosts had lost Tommy Searle in a nasty first lap crash in a damp Nations debut for the teenager but he finished 9th for their best finish in the next moto. Carl Nunn struggled with a 450 he had hardly ridden and Billy Mackenzie caused the crowd to erupt in the final race as he led for half a lap in the formative stages but a crash and a stall would drop the Yamaha man to 10th as Britain had to be content with 6th in the final ranking.

Stefan Everts aced Moto3 after disputing the lead with David Philippaerts (450 mounted) and Stewart. He was too quick for the American as the race drew to a close and the World Supercross Champion eased off. Everts would be denied a sixth Nations win but it is unlikely that anyone will repeat his achievement of fourteen podiums from fourteen appearances. The Rinaldi Yamaha rider had decided that a complete break from the World Championship was going to be too hard to negotiate and took part in a KTM press conference that caught the paddock on the hop Saturday afternoon as the Austrians propositioned the Belgian as their new Race Director for the internalised 2007 MX1 and MX2 squads. Yamaha were smarting with the decision and after such a strong association with six titles in six fantastic years the breakaway did seem a bold decision by the outgoing World Champ. He maintained that the offer of a new role and fresh challenge was too good to refuse.

Festivities began Sunday night with Team USA filling the Alpinestars hospitality unit (that had also seen World Superbike Champion Troy Corser mingling) and had the joint jumping. The rest of the paddock also breathed easy. The finale of a long season had arrived. There was a palpable air of relief and relaxation but also a tinge of sadness that 2006 had come to an end. The community broke apart for the last time and for a winter break of more than five months before it would all start again.

2006 had been the year of '72', without a doubt. Pourcel, Cairoli, Rattray and Philippaerts provided ample supporting roles and Josh Coppins made a fair bid for a slice of a well-fortified Yamaha MX1 limelight. With Everts now leaving the record books in peace, the remaining brigade in the MX1 category featured a crop of young and interesting characters for a fresh cast and another prospect of captivating motocross nearing the end of the decade.

Stefan Everts...
...the legend

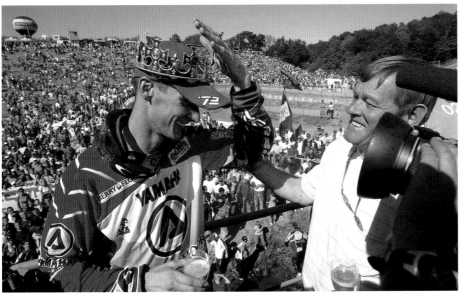

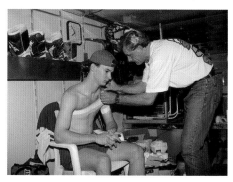

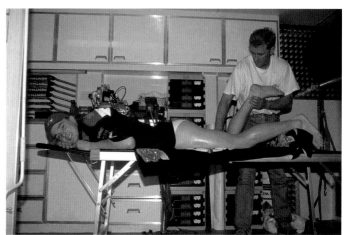

Behind the scenes

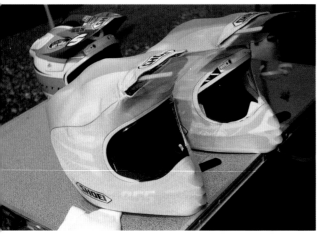

YURI DANESI (I) TECHNICAL SUPPORT
MARC DEFRAINE (B) TECHNICAL SUPPORT
dressed by ACERBIS REPUBLIK

MX WORLD CHAMPIONSHIP 06

ŁULDER		
BELLPUIG	(B)	
AGUEDA	(E)	02 Apr
TEUTSCHENTHAL	(P)	16 Apr
SUGO	(D)	23 Apr
SEVLIEVO	(J)	07 May
MONTEVARCHI	(BG)	21 May
MATTERLEY BASIN	(I)	04 Jun
UDDEVALLA	(GB)	11 Jun
SUN CITY	(S)	18 Jun
LOKET	(ZA)	02 Jul
NAMUR	(CZ)	16 Jul
DESERT MARTIN	(B)	30 Jul
LIEROP	(IRL)	06 Aug
ERNEE	(NL)	27 Aug
	(F)	03 Sep
		17 Sep

MOTOCROSS of NATIONS
MATTERLEY BASIN (GB) 24 Sep

Fire Mover F·750 SUPER DUTY

MX1 FIM MOTOCROSS WORLD CHAMPIONSHIP

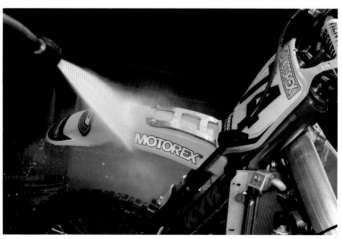

MX1 Results

Pos.	Rider	Nat.	Bike	Total	BEL		SPA		POR		GER		JPN	
1	EVERTS Stefan	BEL	YAMAHA	739	22	25	20	25	25	25	25	25	25	25
2	STRIJBOS Kevin	BEL	SUZUKI	529	13	20	25	2	18	20	22	18	9	18
3	RAMON Steve	BEL	SUZUKI	483	18	16	15	20	14	0	12	16	18	22
4	DE DYCKER Ken	BEL	HONDA	464	16	14	16	15	20	16	16	20	22	13
5	LEOK Tanel	EST	KAWASAKI	443	20	18	22	22	15	18	15	22	20	9
6	BARRAGAN Jonathan	SPA	KTM	376	15	12	18	14	16	22	20	0	13	20
7	COPPINS Joshua	NZL	HONDA	330	-	-	-	-	-	-	-	-	-	-
8	PRIEM Manuel	BEL	YAMAHA	278	0	9	8	13	8	15	8	11	12	15
9	LEURET Pascal	FRA	HONDA	267	14	11	10	12	6	13	13	14	-	-
10	NOBLE James	GBR	HONDA	226	4	10	12	3	13	0	0	7	14	14
11	MELOTTE Cédric	BEL	YAMAHA	224	12	13	11	18	12	0	18	0	15	6
12	GARCIA VICO Javier	SPA	HONDA	201	10	0	5	10	10	10	0	12	3	0
13	CROCKARD Gordon	IRL	HONDA	173	-	-	0	-	9	8	0	0	-	-
14	PYRHONEN Antti	FIN	TM	168	8	6	9	5	3	11	7	6	6	8
15	BILL Julien	SUI	YAMAHA	167	0	0	13	9	4	14	14	13	10	0
16	VAN DAELE Marvin	BEL	HONDA	155	5	7	2	8	5	4	11	8	11	16
17	JORGENSEN Brian	DEN	HONDA	144	0	8	0	11	7	1	10	15	16	0
18	AVIS Wyatt	RSA	KTM	120	7	0	-	-	0	12	0	2	-	-
19	NEMETH Kornel	HUN.	SUZUKI	106	-	-	-	-	-	-	-	-	-	-
20	THEYBERS Danny	BEL	SUZUKI	102	6	0	7	6	0	7	4	9	8	11
21	TORTELLI Sébastien	FRA	KTM	99	25	22	14	16	22	0	-	-	-	-
22	FREIBERGS Lauris	LAT	SUZUKI	87	0	3	0	0	1	9	-	-	-	-
23	SALVINI Alex	ITA	SUZUKI	83	0	0	4	0	0	6	6	-	-	-
24	VERHOEVEN Bas	NED	KAWASAKI	73	9	5	-	0	0	0	0	0	-	-
25	DESALLE Clément	BEL	SUZUKI	70	-	-	-	0	0	0	1	0	-	-
26	LINDHE Jonny	SWE	KTM	47	0	0	6	0	-	5	2	1	5	4
27	JONES Mark	GBR	HONDA	43	-	-	-	-	-	-	-	-	-	-
28	SWORD Stephen	GBR	KAWASAKI	40	11	15	0	-	11	3	-	-	-	-
29	FEDERICI Claudio	ITA	KAWASAKI	34	2	0	0	0	2	0	5	0	-	-
30	BOBKOVS Aigars	LAT	HONDA	31	0	0	0	7	0	0	9	5	-	-
31	NORLEN Marcus	SWE	SUZUKI	30	-	1	-	-	-	-	-	0	-	-
32	SALAETS Kristof	BEL	YAMAHA	29	-	-	-	-	0	2	-	-	-	-
33	KOVALAINEN Marko	FIN	HONDA	27	-	-	0	0	-	-	3	0	-	-
34	BRADSHAW Neville	RSA	SUZUKI	23	-	-	-	-	-	-	-	-	-	-
35	DUGMORE Collin	RSA	KAWASAKI	22	-	-	-	-	-	-	0	10	-	-
36	NARITA Akira	JPN	YAMAHA	19	-	-	-	-	-	-	-	-	7	12
37	BEGGI Christian	ITA	HONDA	19	-	-	-	-	-	-	-	-	-	-
38	JELEN Roman	SLO	SUZUKI	15	-	-	0	0	-	-	0	4	-	-
39	HUCKLEBRIDGE Mark	GBR	KAWASAKI	15	3	2	3	4	-	0	0	3	-	0
40	KAGA Shinichi	JPN	SUZUKI	12	-	-	-	-	-	-	-	-	2	10

MAKES

Pos.	Make			Total	BEL		SPA		POR		GER		JPN	
1	YAMAHA			739	22	25	20	25	25	25	25	25	25	25
2	SUZUKI			580	18	16	15	20	18	20	22	18	18	22
3	HONDA			566	16	14	16	15	20	16	16	20	22	13
4	KAWASAKI			450	20	18	22	22	15	18	15	22	20	9
5	KTM			440	25	22	18	14	16	22	20	-	13	20
6	TM			168	8	6	9	5	3	11	7	6	6	8

BLG		ITA		GBR		SWE		RSA		CZE		BEL		IRL		NED		FRA	
25	25	25	25	25	25	25	25	25	25	25	25	25	25	25	22	25	25	25	25
22	22	22	22	18	22	15	20	12	16	15	22	13	18	18	16	15	18	20	18
20	20	18	18	7	20	18	22	20	20	18	16	20	20	10	0	20	16	14	15
14	15	20	14	22	14	13	12	16	14	16	15	16	3	20	18	16	9	16	13
12	18	14	20	15	18	16	0	18	18	13	12	0	10	9	13	18	0	18	20
0	0	16	0	9	15	22	0	8	15	20	18	0	-	13	20	12	20	22	16
-	-	-	-	20	16	20	16	22	22	22	20	22	22	22	25	22	22	15	22
7	0	2	12	6	10	0	10	13	9	10	11	8	13	14	15	13	15	4	7
16	14	11	13	12	0	0	0	14	13	12	4	14	14	5	7	0	5	11	9
0	2	0	10	10	9	11	13	0	6	14	9	10	15	0	12	2	2	12	12
0	-	13	0	16	13	10	0	15	0	5	13	18	16	-	-	-	-	-	-
11	13	15	16	13	11	12	14	7	-	-	-	12	12	-	-	-	-	5	0
10	4	8	1	14	-	14	18	6	10	1	14	15	5	16	0	0	-	9	11
5	8	0	9	3	0	5	7	10	12	0	0	4	6	12	11	0	0	3	4
13	0	12	5	11	8	8	11	11	11	0	-	-	-	-	-	-	-	-	-
8	12	0	11	0	12	7	0	-	-	-	-	-	-	0	2	9	8	1	8
18	16	3	15	-	-	9	2	-	-	0	-	-	-	-	-	0	-	13	0
15	7	0	3	-	-	-	-	9	8	11	10	11	11	0	-	0	14	0	0
-	-	-	-	-	-	4	15	-	-	7	8	0	0	15	14	7	12	10	14
2	0	5	8	5	0	6	0	-	-	0	0	9	9	-	-	-	-	-	-
-	-	-	-	-	-	-	-	-	-	-	-	-	-	-	-	-	-	-	-
1	5	9	7	4	0	0	9	-	-	6	1	0	2	0	9	6	13	-	2
4	11	10	6	0	3	0	5	-	-	8	7	3	0	0	0	8	0	2	0
3	6	0	0	0	1	-	0	-	-	3	0	0	7	0	4	14	11	0	10
9	9	6	0	0	0	2	3	-	-	9	0	7	1	0	0	5	6	7	5
0	0	0	0	0	4	3	-	-	-	0	0	0	0	3	10	3	1	-	-
-	-	-	-	8	5	-	-	-	-	-	-	-	-	6	0	0	10	8	6
-	-	-	-	-	-	-	-	-	-	-	-	-	-	-	-	-	-	-	-
6	10	-	0	2	7	0	-	-	-	0	0	-	-	-	-	-	-	-	-
0	3	-	-	0	2	0	1	-	-	0	3	-	-	-	-	1	0	-	-
-	1	-	-	-	-	-	-	-	-	-	-	-	-	2	8	11	7	-	-
0	0	1	0	-	-	-	-	-	-	-	-	-	-	8	5	10	3	-	-
-	-	-	-	0	0	1	8	-	-	4	6	5	0	0	0	0	0	0	0
-	-	-	-	1	6	0	6	-	-	-	-	-	-	4	6	-	-	-	-
-	-	-	-	-	-	-	-	5	7	-	-	-	-	-	-	-	-	-	-
-	-	-	-	-	-	-	-	-	-	-	-	-	-	-	-	-	-	-	-
-	-	-	-	-	-	-	-	-	-	-	-	0	8	11	0	-	-	0	0
-	-	7	4	-	-	-	-	-	-	-	-	-	-	-	-	-	-	-	-
-	-	-	-	-	-	-	-	-	-	-	-	-	-	-	-	-	-	-	-
-	-	-	-	-	-	-	-	-	-	-	-	-	-	-	-	-	-	-	-
25	25	25	25	25	25	25	25	25	25	25	25	25	25	25	22	25	25	25	25
22	22	22	22	18	22	18	22	20	20	15	22	20	20	18	16	20	16	20	18
18	16	20	14	22	14	20	16	22	22	22	20	22	22	22	25	22	22	15	22
12	18	14	20	15	18	16	-	18	18	13	12	-	10	9	13	14	11	18	20
15	7	16	-	9	15	22	-	8	15	20	18	11	11	13	20	12	20	22	16
5	8	-	9	3	-	5	7	10	12	-	-	4	6	12	11	-	-	3	4

ROUND 1 Tortelli Everts Leok

ROUND 2 Leok Everts Ramon

ROUND 3 Barragan Everts Strijbos

ROUND 4 Strijbos Everts Leok

ROUND 5 Ramon Everts DeDyker

ROUND 6 Strijbos Everts Ramon

ROUND 7 Strijbos Everts Ramon

ROUND 8 Strijbos Everts Coppins

ROUND 9 Ramon Everts Coppins

ROUND 10 Coppins Everts Ramon

ROUND 11 Coppins Everts Barragan

ROUND 12 Coppins Everts Ramon

ROUND 13 Everts Coppins DeDyker

ROUND 14 Coppins Everts Ramon

ROUND 15 Leok Everts Strijbos

ROUND 1 De Reuver Rattray Gundersen

ROUND 2 MacKenzie Rattray De Reuver

ROUND 3 C Pourcel Rattray Cairoli

ROUND 4 De Reuver C Pourcel Rattray

ROUND 5 Cairoli MacKenzie De Reuver

ROUND 6 Philippaerts De Reuver C Pourcel

ROUND 7 Cairoli Philippaerts C Pourcel

ROUND 8 Cairoli Philippaerts Searle

ROUND 9 C Pourcel Philippaerts Searle

ROUND 10 Rattray Cairoli Nunn

ROUND 11 C Pourcel Philippaerts Nunn

ROUND 12 C Pourcel Cairoli S Pourcel

ROUND 13 C Pourcel Rattray Cairoli

ROUND 14 Cairoli C Pourcel Rattray

ROUND 15 Philippaerts Cairoli C Pourcel

MX2 Results

Pos.	Rider	Nat.	Bike	Total	BEL		SPA		POR		GER		JPN	
1	POURCEL Christophe	FRA	KAWASAKI	581	14	18	18	14	22	22	25	25	22	16
2	CAIROLI Antonio	ITA	YAMAHA	563	6	22	-	25	25	11	16	14	18	25
3	PHILIPPAERTS David	ITA	KTM	480	25	8	11	15	15	0	8	18	16	4
4	RATTRAY Tyla	RSA	KTM	475	20	25	16	22	20	25	18	20	15	-
5	DE REUVER Marc	NED	KTM	408	18	20	20	16	18	16	22	22	20	22
6	NUNN Carl	GBR	KTM	377	13	11	14	9	16	13	9	10	9	15
7	GONCALVES Rui	POR	KTM	325	8	16	0	18	12	0	4	12	8	12
8	SEARLE Tommy	GBR	KAWASAKI	315	12	10	10	0	11	14	10	11	13	14
9	MACKENZIE Billy	GBR	YAMAHA	302	0	12	13	20	14	15	15	16	25	20
10	POURCEL Sébastien	FRA	KAWASAKI	298	16	13	15	0	0	8	0	0	11	7
11	SWANEPOEL Gareth	RSA	KAWASAKI	286	5	0	0	10	10	12	12	6	14	18
12	CHIODI Alessio	ITA	YAMAHA	229	15	0	22	11	13	20	20	0	5	5
13	GUNDERSEN Kenneth	NOR	YAMAHA	223	22	15	25	2	9	0	14	2	12	10
14	MONNI Manuel	ITA	KTM	196	3	0	3	5	4	3	5	8	3	8
15	LEOK Aigar	EST	YAMAHA	160	7	6	-	-	0	0	13	7	0	13
16	GUARNERI Davide	ITA	YAMAHA	153	10	9	0	13	0	6	0	15	0	11
17	SEISTOLA Matti	FIN	HONDA	150	0	4	9	0	8	5	7	3	-	-
18	BOISSIERE Anthony	FRA	YAMAHA	112	-	-	5	3	7	9	11	5	10	0
19	RENET Pierre Alexandre	FRA	HONDA	106	2	5	0	7	6	1	0	4	-	-
20	NAGL Maximilian	GER	KTM	103	4	2	-	0	7	3	13	7	9	
21	CAPS Patrick	BEL	HONDA	96	9	3	8	8	0	18	0	0	-	-
22	SEGUY Luigi	FRA	YAMAHA	94	1	7	12	12	-	10	0	9	6	6
23	AUBIN Nicolas	FRA	KTM	87	-	-	0	6	5	4	0	0	-	-
24	CAMPANO Carlos	SPA	KTM	70	0	0	0	0	-	0	0	0	-	-
25	SCHIFFER Marcus	GER	KTM	60	0	0	7	0	3	0	0	0	-	-
26	CHURCH Tom	GBR	KAWASAKI	46	-	-	-	-	-	-	-	-	-	-
27	DOUGAN Jason	GBR	HONDA	36	0	1	6	0	-	-	6	0	-	-
28	MEO Antoine	FRA	HONDA	30	11	14	2	0	0		-	-	-	-
29	BOOG Xavier	FRA	YAMAHA	28	0	0	4	4	-	-	-	-	-	-
30	VERBRUGGEN Dennis	BEL	YAMAHA	22	-	-	-	-	-	-	-	-	-	-
31	ROELANTS Joel	BEL	KTM	19	-	-	-	-	-	-	-	-	-	-
32	KOHUT Martin	SVK	HONDA	17	-	-	-	-	-	-	-	-	-	-
33	SIMPSON Shaun	GBR	HONDA	17	0	0	-	-	0	0	-	-	-	-
34	WING Jonas	SWE	KTM	17	-	-	0	0	2	0	1	1	-	-
35	VAN VIJFEIJKEN Rob	NED	YAMAHA	15	-	-	-	-	-	-	-	-	-	-
36	BONINI Mateo	ITA	YAMAHA	9	-	-	-	-	-	-	-	-	-	-
37	REMES Eero	FIN	HONDA	9	-	-	-	-	-	-	-	-	-	-
38	MOSSINI Fabio	RSM	SUZUKI	9	-	-	-	-	-	-	2	0	-	-
39	NAUDE Sasha	RSA	YAMAHA	9	-	-	-	-	-	-	-	-	-	-
40	CARLSSON Johan	SWE	YAMAHA	8	-	-	-	-	0	0	-	-	-	-

MAKES

Pos.	Make			Total	BEL		SPA		POR		GER		JPN	
1	KTM			648	20	25	16	22	20	25	22	22	20	22
2	YAMAHA			583	22	15	13	20	25	11	15	16	25	20
3	KAWASAKI			583	14	18	18	14	22	22	25	25	22	16
4	HONDA			228	11	14	8	8	-	18	7	3	-	2
5	SUZUKI			16	-	-	-	-	-	-	2	-	4	-

BLG		ITA		GBR		SWE		RSA		CZE		BEL		IRL		NED		FRA	
22	18	18	20	22	9	20	25	11	18	15	22	20	22	20	18	20	25	22	18
25	0	22	22	15	25	22	9	20	25	10	25	25	25	22	14	25	20	25	25
20	20	25	25	25	22	25	22	25	0	22	20	22	0	14	20	13	0	20	20
16	22	16	0	4	6	16	0	22	22	25	0	4	18	25	25	22	22	14	15
15	25	12	0	0	4	18	16	0	0	12	18	16	8	13	22	0	0	13	22
10	14	7	9	10	12	10	14	16	20	20	16	10	20	8	0	12	16	18	16
2	15	10	15	9	16	12	0	9	15	9	7	13	14	18	13	15	18	11	14
3	1	6	14	13	20	14	20	15	13	16	14	-	-	10	0	18	14	9	10
0	10	0	8	20	13	0	12	5	10	3	15	14	4	5	12	0	0	12	9
18	16	20	16	11	18	0	11	13	14	5	13	18	16	16	16	0	0	7	0
12	2	15	18	14	0	15	18	18	11	14	12	0	15	12	15	8	0	-	-
-	-	3	10	8	11	13	8	12	9	18	8	-	-	-	-	-	-	10	8
0	11	13	4	16	15	11	13	-	-	0	3	3	0	15	-	0	-	8	0
9	13	9	0	6	10	-	10	10	16	7	11	12	12	9	7	-	-	0	13
7	0	11	0	0	-	9	0	-	-	2	2	7	13	11	10	16	15	4	7
13	3	14	0	18	0	0	15	14	12	-	-	0	0	-	-	-	-	0	0
5	0	8	12	0	8	0	0	-	-	11	5	11	9	6	8	10	12	5	4
11	5	-	-	7	14	-	-	-	-	0	0	5	6	-	-	1	7	0	6
0	4	4	6	5	7	1	5	-	-	0	4	8	11	2	0	0	9	3	12
-	-	-	-	-	-	-	-	-	-	0	6	15	0	7	-	14	10	1	5
-	-	-	-	-	-	-	-	-	-	13	9	9	0	3	0	-	-	16	0
8	12	0	11	-	-	-	-	-	-	-	-	-	-	-	-	-	-	-	-
14	0	-	-	12	0	8	6	-	-	-	-	-	-	1	0	0	5	15	11
6	0	5	13	0	0	5	7	-	-	8	10	0	10	0	1	-	-	2	3
4	9	2	2	-	-	-	-	-	-	-	-	-	-	0	11	9	13	-	-
0	6	-	-	0	0	-	4	8	8	6	1	-	-	0	5	0	2	6	0
-	-	-	-	1	0	4	0	7	7	4	0	-	-	-	-	-	-	-	-
-	-	0	3	-	-	-	-	-	-	-	-	-	-	-	-	-	-	-	-
1	0	0	0	0	3	-	1	-	-	-	-	1	3	0	6	4	0	0	1
-	-	-	-	-	-	-	-	-	-	0	0	0	5	0	0	6	11	0	0
-	-	-	-	-	-	-	-	-	-	-	-	0	0	4	4	11	0	-	-
0	8	-	-	-	-	-	-	-	-	-	-	-	-	0	9	-	-	-	-
0	7	0	0	2	2	-	-	-	-	0	0	6	0	-	-	-	-	-	-
-	-	1	1	0	1	6	3	-	-	-	-	0	1	0	0	0	-	-	-
-	-	-	-	-	-	-	-	-	-	-	-	-	-	-	-	7	8	-	-
-	-	-	-	-	-	0	0	-	-	0	0	0	7	0	0	0	0	0	2
-	-	-	-	-	-	7	2	-	-	-	-	-	-	-	-	-	-	-	-
-	-	0	7	-	-	0	0	-	-	0	0	-	-	-	-	-	-	-	-
-	-	-	-	-	-	-	-	3	6	-	-	-	-	-	-	-	-	-	-
-	-	0	0	-	-	-	-	-	-	-	-	-	-	-	-	2	6	-	-
20	20	25	25	25	22	25	22	22	22	22	20	10	20	25	25	22	22	20	20
25	-	22	22	15	25	22	9	20	25	10	25	25	25	22	14	25	20	25	25
22	18	18	20	13	20	20	25	18	11	15	22	20	22	20	18	20	25	22	18
-	8	8	12	5	7	7	2	7	7	13	9	11	9	6	8	10	12	16	-
-	-	-	7	-	-	3	-	-	-	-	-	-	-	-	-	-	-	-	-